EFFECTIVE REPORTING

by
Trudy H. Bers
with Jeffrey A. Seybert

RIR Editor
Richard D. Howard

THE ASSOCIATION FOR INSTITUTIONAL RESEARCH
Number Twelve
Resources in Institutional Research

ISBN 1882393-08-2

Table of Contents

Introduction

This monograph came about for a variety of reasons. One is the strong interest shown by the Association for Institutional Research (AIR) members in the subject of graphic depictions of data and effective reporting. A number of indicators of this interest exist. In June 1986, Edward Tufte presented a keynote address at the AIR Annual Forum in Orlando, FL, about the use of graphics to portray data and information. Using a variety of illustrations, few from higher education, he captured his audience and held their attention to a degree rarely observed in any address to an audience of 1,000 people. Tufte's message was actually quite simple, and is presented cogently in his 1983 book *The Visual Display of Quantitative Information*: data graphics are paragraphs about data and should be treated as such. The implication of this concept is that graphics must be integrated with the text, illustrating key points or providing data and information in a format that makes them easier to grasp and understand than the written word permits (p. 28). Tufte's keynote address continues to be among the most memorable presented to the Association.

A second indicator is the continuing attraction of pre-Forum workshops and the module about Effective Reporting included in the AIR Foundations Institute, and the movement of state and regional institutional research associations to schedule similar sessions at their annual meetings. Jeff Seybert developed the original effective reporting workshop, which has also been presented by Harriott Calhoun and Trudy Bers. A third indicator is the positive reception of 1995 AIR Forum participants to the keynote address by Stephen Kosslyn, who demonstrated, through graphic displays, how our eyes and brain receive and interpret visual symbols.

A second reason for writing this monograph is the persistent disappointment, even complaints, among conference attendees at all types of meetings about the poor quality of graphics and visual presentations used by presenters. This concern spans disciplines, scope of conferences (local, national or international), size of audiences, and subject of presentations. Despite the widespread availability and relative low cost of sophisticated graphics and presentation software that can generate high quality images in a matter of moments, a surprising number of presenters continue to use dull, small type, barely readable images that resemble pages created on old typewriters. Graphic representations of data are little better, often employing shading or patterns that hinder rather than help understanding.

A third reason is the lack of a short, readily available, usable guide for institution researchers. Most researchers' expertise is in designing and implementing research, not in presenting data and information from that research. However, the success and overall quality of work they do are affected by how the work is presented as well as the substance. Few researchers have the time, resources, or motivation to research the literature or to attend professional meetings related to graphic design or writing prose. However, based on the popularity and positive evaluations of programs about reporting, which we noted above, it is clear they want to improve what they produce and to learn more about how to accomplish this goal.[1]

A quite different reason for developing this work is the increasing attention being given to the critical thinking skill of graphicacy, the ability to understand graphic displays (Wainer, 1992). Wainer suggests there are three basic levels of questions that charts can be used to answer. We have adapted them using examples from higher education.

- Very elementary questions, such as "What is the average student grade point average?"

- Intermediate level questions that involve trends, such as "How have student grade point averages changed from 1980 to 1995?"

- Higher level questions that involve relationships among variables and more sophisticated reasoning, such as "What grade point averages are expected for various student ethnic groups, based on what variables?"

Our last reason is more personal. During the past few years, we each have received positive feedback for some of the graphic depictions of data and information we have used in our presentations and reports. We have learned that when our work, whether formal reports or informal presentations, is enhanced by high quality graphic displays, it is received more favorably, conveys information more forcefully, and holds audience attention more strongly than works that use text alone or pedantic black and white tables or graphs. It has, frankly, been challenging and fun to create visual displays, especially because the overall merit of our work has improved.

We have also noticed that brief reports, especially those that contain bulleted points, questions and answers rather than didactic presentations, and clear headings and subheadings to guide the reader, garner more attention and generate more conversation than long, formal reports of many pages. The analytic, technical, and data-intensive tables we, as institutional researchers, so admire, do not travel well to most colleagues, and certainly are little appreciated by audiences outside of higher education.

Most of what we learned has occurred as a result of our culling through existing literature, listening to and watching presentations, trial and error in creating graphics and reports, and talking to others. Of special value for one of us – Trudy Bers – was a presentation done by her colleague, James Krauss, at Oakton Community College. Krauss, a professor in the art department, offers a workshop/seminar titled "Taming the Blackboard Jungle," in which he offers instructors new ideas and insights to make their classroom presentations more visually effective.

Putting together what we learned in this document forced us to review, rethink, and reorganize our scattered information and, in the process, we hope, develop a resource that will be useful for others.

This work focuses on several types of presentations. The first type of presentation is the written report. Usually researchers' major focus in preparing reports is on the contents, not on alternative ways for presenting information, the report's appearance, or the audiences to which a report is directed. These are critical attributes, however, and markedly affect how our work is received, interpreted, and used.

The second type of presentation is graphic displays, or charts. Often included within reports, and so germane to them, graphics also stand alone as a topic to be considered. Following Mims (1987), we use the term *chart* as the most generic term for graphic displays. Charts can a) present words in an organized fashion, such as an organization chart; b) present data in an organized or symbolic fashion, such as in a bar chart or map; c) present text or symbols to depict an object, concept or process, such as in a flowchart; or d) present numerical, verbal or symbolic information in a table. The term *graph* usually is restricted to statistical charts. Web pages are a form of graphic display.

The third type of presentation is oral. Not a speech communications text, this monograph does, however, present some key principles for enhancing oral presentations, whether they take place in fairly informal settings such as committee meetings, at professional conferences, or to audiences drawn primarily from outside higher education such as legislators or community groups.

Together, written reports, graphical displays, and oral presentations comprise the dominant means by which researchers convey their work to others. Effective communication requires, at the outset, thought, planning, and consideration of the "others" to whom communications are directed. We begin this monograph with some general observations about the reporting process overall, then consider more specific aspects of effective communications.

Trudy Bers and Jeffrey Seybert

Electronic Appendix

With this volume of the *Resources in Institutional Research* book series, the AIR Publications Committee is introducing the use of the Web to enhance the contents of its publications. A major component of this volume is devoted to the development and use of effective graphics in presenting comparative and trend data. As the authors, Trudy Bers and Jeffrey Seybert, point out, the decision to use or not to use color in a presentation or report may influence the audience's perceptions of the presenter's professionalism, in spite of the content quality.

While the graphics presented in this book accurately reflect the points that the authors discuss, we believe that providing color versions of the same graphics will enhance the illustrations. As such, the graphics were created and posted at: http://airweb.org/publications/ EffectiveReporting.html. We think that the graphic illustrations contained in this "electronic appendix" will increase the usefulness of the book.

Richard D. Howard
RIR Editor

About the Authors

Trudy H. Bers is Senior Director of Research, Curriculum and Planning at Oakton College, Illinois. She received her bachelor of arts and doctorate in political science from the University of Illinois-Urbana, and also has master's degrees from Columbia University in public law and government and the Kellogg Graduate School of Management at Northwestern University in marketing and organizational behavior. She has been active in a number of national organizations, serving as the Association for Institutional Research president in 1995-96 and as the chairperson of the National Postsecondary Education Cooperative in 1998.

Jeffrey A. Seybert is Director of Research, Evaluation, and Instructional Development at Johnson County Community College, Overland Park, KS. He has a bachelor's degree in psychology from California State University-Long Beach, master's and doctoral degrees in psychology from the University of Oklahoma, and a master's degree in public administration from the University of Missouri-Kansas City. Jeff has been active in several professional organizations including the Association for Institutional Research, the National Council for Research and Planning, and the Mid-America Association for Institutional Research.

The authors want to recognize Glenn Puffer for his work on the graphics and charts for this book. Mr. Puffer is a doctoral student in Adult and Higher Education at Montana State University. His dissertation topic is concerned with distance delivered programs and their perceived value when compared to traditional on-campus programs by hiring agents in industry. He is currently serving as the Assistant Dean of Students at Montana State University.

Chapter 1
The Reporting Process

Effective reporting is a step-by-step process that entails careful consideration of a variety of issues. While many issues can be anticipated and addressed at the outset of a project, often new issues arise as a project unfolds. Sometimes issues grow out of a prior stage or findings of a project, but sometimes they arise through external events, unexpected demands, changes in key personnel or audiences, political situations, or a host of other factors. In general, the smaller the project, in terms of time, resource requirements, range of audiences, and potential impact, the less likely it is that unanticipated issues will affect the project. While the reporting process described below suggests a linear and neat order of work, in reality effective reporting requires researchers to remain flexible through the course of a project.

The Reporting Process

Effective reporting typically involves major steps, usually sequential but sometimes requiring circling back to prior steps to refine, redirect, clarify, or otherwise revise a report to accommodate emerging demands or changing circumstances. Laying out major steps forms a template and useful checklist for researchers. Major steps include:

1. Determining the clients, purpose, and audiences for the report. The client is the person or office requesting or commissioning the report; the purpose is the reason for their making the request and the use to which the report might be put; and the audience comprise the client as well as other individuals or groups that will receive the report, whether written or oral. Determining client, purpose, and audiences is a related task because the client frequently determines the purpose of a report, and the initial purpose for preparing a report may influence audiences identified as report recipients. Is the report intended to inform, to persuade, or to serve both purposes? Is the report being prepared to comply with external reporting requirements, to fulfull public relations needs, to meet accreditation or program certification criteria, to present basic information about the institution, to investigate a narrowly defined issue or problem, or as support for planning or decision making, or as a historical

record of a program or process? These are just a sample of purposes that can be served by a report. Frequently a report must serve multiple purposes, which may not be compatible. For example, a report on the retention and success of students enrolled in distance education courses might be expected by one segment of audiences to illustrate the association between student support services and student retention/success, thereby implying the need for increased student support resources for this population, whereas another segment of audiences might expect the report to demonstrate the cost-effectiveness and productivity of distance education courses.

In the case of major or new reports, researchers may find it beneficial to interview those who made the request and to clarify with them what they perceive to be the report's purpose and audience. The requester does not always ask for exactly what he or she wants to know. For example, a vice president may ask how many part-time faculty teach at the institution, but the real subject of interest is whether the number of part-time faculty has changed over time and whether part-time are replacing full-time faculty. Such interviews can serve as useful sessions in which to educate requesters about existing reports and data sources, possible additional purposes and audiences that may find the particular report of value, and the resources required for conducting the project. The issue of resources is of critical importance for institutional research projects overall, not just for effective reporting. Resources impact reporting in a number of ways. It may be costly to obtain, combine, manipulate, and interpret data. It may also be costly to prepare elaborate presentation materials as compared to simple manuscripts that are word processed. "Who will pay, and how much?" is an uncomfortable but necessary question to raise, because the answer to that question may well determine whether or not a project moves forward as originally planned, and in what formats it will ultimately be presented.

2. Determining what data and information are available or must be gathered to satisfy the request. Even after data are collected, researchers may find it helpful to reconsider and validate the client, purpose, and audiences before beginning to analyze data or write the report. Institutional researchers sometimes find themselves immersed in the detail and data of a report, forgetting its main

purpose and audience, and even who requested the report in the first place. Sophisticated analyses and pages of text and charts satisfy researchers, but can render the report less appreciated by the audience and less satisfactory in serving the purpose for which the report was generated.

3. The third step in effective reporting is to select the type of report, which is again influenced by the client, purpose and audiences. Chapter 3 contains a discussion of common types of reports prepared by institutional researchers.

4. The fourth step is to select the report format. In brief, reports may be written, oral, electronic, or combinations. Written reports may be comprehensive documents containing all or most components outlined in Chapter 3, brief newsletters or bulletins, formal memoranda meant for internal distribution only, informal working papers or briefings usually intended as raw material, or draft documents to further the work of a committee or higher level administrator, or tables and charts of data expected to stand on their own without narrative. Like written reports, oral reports may be formal or informal; may be enhanced with the use of visuals such as overhead transparencies or electronic presentations; supplemented with written handouts distributed either before or after the presentation. Electronic formats are still relatively new. Though in some sense they are like written presentations, with the image appearing first on a screen rather than paper, reports presented through electronic communications do require special consideration with respect to such issues as readability on an LCD screen, rapidity of downloading, use of sound or motion, and layout and design.

5. The fifth step in effective reporting is deciding how to depict data and information. This decision is influenced not just by the client, purpose, audiences, type and format of the report, but also by the nature of the data and information. Some data and information are most effectively transmitted through narratives, some through tables, and some through charts. Sophisticated graphics software packages are temptingly useful tools that permit multi-color, multi-dimensional, multi-font presentations of data and information decorated with symbols, cartoons, pictures, and even sound or motion.

6. The next step in effective reporting is to actually produce the report; that is, to perform data analyses and interpretations, write the report itself, prepare tables and charts, compile glossaries, appendices, exhibits and other attachments. Part of report production includes packaging the report: binding, cover style, paperstock, two or more color print, inclusion of photographs, and so forth. For oral reports, production may involve developing an outline or writing a script, preparing visual aids and handouts, and rehearsing the oral presentation. Electronic reports require encoding and perhaps reformatting of text or graphics to better suit electronic transmission.

7. The final step in effective reporting is dissemination. Key considerations in disseminating a report are defining recipients; deciding whether or not there should be a cover letter or memo and, if so, from whom; and selecting distribution channels such as campus mail, regular mail, Web sites, and distribution at a meeting or event.

Probably the most frustrating aspect of research is seeing work go unused. Clients and audiences must be provided with the information they need, in ways that are understandable to them, and in time to be useful. The degree to which the results of research are used is very often a direct function of how effectively they are communicated. Accurately determining client and audience needs and levels of sophistication, with regard to research data and information, is crucial to the utility and effectiveness of reporting.

Parenthetically, it should be noted that most non-researchers fail to discriminate between data and information. Data are value-free facts. Information is data set within a context: data combined and manipulated with other data. For example, projections are information based on data from prior years set within the context of current and future periods. This distinction need not be made explicit in a report, but occasionally it may be helpful to gently remind the client and audiences about the difference.

Research professionals are comfortable with quantitative data, statistical analyses, and relatively complex ways of presenting data: e.g., data-rich tables. Thus, expertise in these areas prompts the production and presentation of reports that are understandable to the researcher, who thinks they accurately and comprehensively reflect the results he or she wishes to communicate. Often, however, clients and audiences are neither very sophisticated nor comfortable with these coins of the researcher's professional realm. Reports that make sense to the research professional may befuddle and even intimidate the audience—they see complex tables, results of statistical analyses, and other professional jargon and their eyes begin to glaze over. At this point, they become lost, and the results of research are probably under-utilized or ignored completely. Therefore, one of the most important tasks in diagnosing audiences' needs also involves diagnosing the level at which they can understand and use what is reported, and then later making sure that the report is presented at the appropriate level. It is the researchers' responsibility, not the audiences', to make sure this happens. Stated differently, it is up to the research professional to pitch the report so that it is consumable for and thus useful to that audience.

Another crucial factor in the usability of reports is their timeliness— reports must be produced and delivered to clients so they have time to absorb the information and to use it for the purpose for which it was intended. The ideal report is aesthetically pleasing, clearly written, based on perfect statistical analyses, contains appropriate tables and graphs, provides incisive and correct interpretations of findings, and includes wise and feasible recommendations. However, if this exemplary report is delivered too late for the client to make use of it, all the work that went into the report is for naught. Perfection delivered late is virtually useless; therefore, reports simply must be delivered in the time frame defined at the initiation of the project.

A Few Words About Writing

This monograph is about effective communication and reporting, not about writing per se. However, the majority of reporting done by institutional researchers is in writing, though few institutional researchers receive formal training in writing. In fact, writing is quite difficult for many researchers, and thus often poses a significant barrier to creating effective, usable reports. Thus some words about writing are in order, though it is important to emphasize that this section is not intended to be a comprehensive review of the principles and techniques of effective writing. Such an exercise lies beyond the scope of this work.

Robert Lucas (1996) has provided some valuable advice to help researchers and other professionals improve both their writing habits and the quality of their technical writing. In his keynote address to the AIR Annual Forum in 1996, Lucas first identified several myths about writing:

- **Writing must be perfect the first time**. In reality, effective writing proceeds in stages, from very rough early drafts through a series of successive improvements. Perfection is the goal at the end of the process, not the beginning.

- **Writing must be inspired and spontaneous**. Good writing is the product of good thinking, which is most often produced by conversation and consultation with colleagues, brainstorming, outlining, and notetaking. It is thus a slow, deliberate process rather than a quick recording of inspiration.

- **Writing proceeds quickly**. Most effective writing evolves in a slow, extended, developmental process over a period of days or weeks, rather than happening all at once.

- **Writing is inherently difficult**. Lucas believes that this myth is a product of training and experience. We believe writing is difficult because we have heard so often that it is, or because we have convinced ourselves that it is as a result of our less-than-successful experiences. In fact, good writing is a skill and, like other skills, can be learned and developed through regular practice. The best way to become more comfortable with writing and to produce better written work is simply to do more of it.

Lucas and others provide a number of suggestions to help individuals become more productive, effective writers. First, write regularly. Set aside regular writing sessions, approximately four per week, ideally separated by no more than 24 to 48 hours. In this way, writing will become a normal, regular part of one's professional routine, rather than looming as a large, momentous, intimidating, dreaded event to be dealt with only occasionally, like a trip to the dentist.

Second, write in small amounts. Lucas recommends 25 to 30 minute sessions. Some good writers like to extend these sessions to an hour or two at most. The point is to write more often, but in shorter bursts. A corollary is to avoid writing in long, extended periods. Do not binge in long, infrequent sessions; again, writing in short, regular sessions is much more effective.

Third, get in the habit of limiting interruptions while writing. Close the door, if possible; have telephone calls held. Mark off regular times on the appointment calendar and dedicate this time solely to writing.

Fourth, prevent writer's block from stopping you. A variety of techniques can be employed to get around the periods when nothing seems to come. For instance, do a "free write" or "brain dump," simply brainstorming on paper, on the computer, or even into a small tape recorder. Gaps and missing information can be filled in later; spelling and rules of grammar may be suspended at this stage. The point is to transmit ideas to paper or tape in a rough draft, understanding that effective material can be culled for subsequent drafts, and whatever does not work can be discarded.

Fifth, share writing early and often, before it goes public. Feedback from different perspectives is invaluable; ask colleagues to read early drafts and incorporate their input as appropriate. An important characteristic of this process is the ability to accept constructive criticism and use it to improve the work. In many institutional research offices, writing is routinely reviewed by two or three staff members, in addition to the author, before the report is distributed publicly.

Finally, consult references about writing and consider, if available, identifying some faculty mentors from the English department to serve as writing consultants. In addition to improved writing, other benefits from working with faculty mentors include strengthened connections between the institutional research office and faculty, and fresh insights into how faculty audiences might perceive or interpret reports.

A Concluding Comment

Effective reporting is dependent on hard work; working and reworking material; and viewing reports, graphics, and oral presentations from the perspective of clients and audiences. While most institutional researchers think of reporting as synonymous with preparing written reports, such documents comprise only one vehicle for conveying research findings. Moreover, researchers are usually trained in the classical, scholarly tradition of independent scholarship. Applied research, which is the domain of institutional researchers, demands additional skills not often considered or developed in graduate programs. For example, applied researchers who report effectively are also able to listen well, translate what they hear into their communications, and recognize and act upon the understanding that what constitutes effective reporting for a research professional may fail to meet the needs of clients and audiences for whom reporting is intended.

Chapter 2
Client and Audience

One of the major considerations in crafting communications is to clearly identify the audience(s) for the message and materials. Indeed, the intended audience can affect even the research design itself, although in this monograph the primary perspective is on the audiences as the recipients of research already completed. Each type of audience will have different levels of interest, expertise, time, background, concerns, technical ability, points of view, and need and willingness to use the data and information. To reach a given audience effectively, its dominant characteristics should be considered when shaping the report's or presentation's contents, format and level of detail.[2]

Types of Audiences

While no audience is uniform in its characteristics, audiences for higher education reports can be differentiated to some extent. The following typology is adapted and expanded from the work of Houp and Pearsall (1992), who described audiences for technical reports similar to many of those prepared in institutional research. They distinguish four types of audiences—executives, experts, technicians, and lay people—with a fifth being a combination of the above, and others. Faculty and Boards of Trustee members constitute additional higher education audiences.

- **Executives**. Executives read reports to make decisions; have more interest in practice than theory; learn from simple charts and plain language; need information on key, often quantitative, indicators such as enrollments or tuition and fee revenues; read selectively, usually skimming and scanning; have self as well as institutional interests; and expect conclusions, implications and recommendations to be expressed clearly. Executives particularly appreciate tables and lists that condense examples into broader headings and that are visually simpler than narrative texts. In higher education, presidents and other upper level officers of the institution comprise the executive audience.

- **Board of trustees members**. Board members read reports to gain information, to shape decisions, and to identify bragging points they can use to promote their institutions. They want a moderate amount of detail, but value summaries and condensations; they often find anecdotes about student and faculty successes to be more compelling and useful than general information or statistics. They appreciate assistance in connecting information about their institutions to the broader constituencies to which they, as board members, relate. Board members sometimes struggle to find the appropriate balance between broad, policy-setting actions and micromanaging their institutions. Thus, reports for them are best targeted to this hypothetical balance point between policy and management.

- **Faculty members**. Faculty want information that is readily understandable and germane to their particular departmental or committee assignments. Some may view themselves as experts in empirical research — even scholars in the field — and may dwell on methodology or arcane points. Others may use more qualitative, even artistic, approaches to conducting research. In any case, they are likely to interpret data and information through the filter of their own experiences at the institution, and chafe at being presented with information that contradicts their view of the academic universe. Depending on the topic, the faculty members' interests and backgrounds, and the political volatility of the topic, faculty may want broad information highlighting major points, or detailed tables and statistical analyses. Providing strong summaries and key findings, in addition to more detailed analyses, will serve the range of faculty, from those who appreciate or even demand the statistical details to those who may have neither the inclination nor the background to interpret technical research.

- **Experts**. Experts read to learn how and why things work; need and want theory; read selectively; bring expertise, background, and technical proficiency to their reading; expect graphics to display results; want new terms defined; expect inferences and conclusions to be clearly expressed, but with caution; and often want lists of references or citations. Middle managers and professional staff in college learning centers, student advisement areas, and career centers are examples of experts.

- **Technicians**. Technicians read reports for how-to information; expect the emphasis to be about application and practical matters;

9

but they may need help with technical concepts and calculations at a level beyond those with which they normally work. More advanced technicians may appreciate some theoretical content. In higher education, experts and technicians are similar, though experts may have more responsibility and authority for implementing programs and services, or serve as assistants to line officials such as presidents or vice presidents.

- **Lay people**. Lay people read a report for general learning and interest; have more interest in practice than theory; may need help with technical concepts and calculations; learn from simple graphics; require background and definitions; and need simplicity. Lay people may be especially receptive to human interest stories and anecdotes about individual students. Parents of potential students, legislators, and staff members who are not higher education experts, and members of the press often constitute lay audiences.

- **Combined audiences.** The combined audience comprises individuals who have characteristics of several of the distinct audiences described above, or a group that contains members of the different audiences, all of whom will receive the identical document. Among the ways to prepare materials for combined audiences are to put more technical material in footnotes or appendices, and to be particularly careful to label each section of the report so that a more technical or theoretical component can be skipped by those not interested in this content.

Audience Point of View and Use of Report

Individuals who perform scholarly or applied research frequently misjudge their audiences, assuming them to be as interested in the topic and the details of the research as are the researchers. Answers to the questions listed below help to clarify the audience point of view and use of a report. The questions should be asked before a report or chart is prepared, and asked periodically during a complex project where the focus might otherwise be lost.

"What do my audiences need to know about this subject?"

"What do my audiences want to know about this subject?"

"What do I want to tell them about this subject?"

"What decisions will or might my audience make based on this report?"

"What other individuals might my primary audience send this report to, even if I haven't intended them to receive the material in this format, or at all?"

"Who else (other audiences) might be interested in the same subject, and will they see the same documents, or others derived from the same research?"

Some Off-The-Record Notes About Audiences

As one considers audiences for a report, some additional observations may be helpful in guiding the presentation preparation. For example, different audiences may want different data and information, even to answer the same questions. Sometimes the same audiences will require several distinct reports, all of which focus on the same general questions, before those individuals will pay attention to or be able to understand the findings and their implications. A certain amount of repetition and redundancy may be essential, particularly if the topic is sensitive or complex.

Sometimes a client, even one who believes most fervently that he or she knows what he or she wants or needs, is confused in reality. In these cases, the researcher may have to assume the role of consultant to help the client clarify the questions being asked, and the array of data and information being sought to address those questions. Simple questions can be fraught with complexity. Consider, for example, the oft-posed question "How many students are enrolled in the College?" Do "students" include continuing education or non-credit students? Should students in distance education or off-site classes be included? What about students taking a semester abroad under the auspices of a different institution? What date should be used in determining enrollment: first day of classes, official census date, date when state reimbursements are determined, end of term? These are but a handful of contingency questions that need to be resolved and clarified before even the simplest question about "enrollment" can be answered. The researcher will probably need to help the client clarify what it is he or she really wants to know, and to elicit the clarification without embarrassing the client.

Even if the client is clear, the audiences may not be. Institutional researchers may need to help audiences clarify questions and understand the complexity of data and information. This process is equally and potentially even more delicate than working with the client because audiences may not receive, nor begin to question, the report until after it is produced and disseminated.

A politically sensitive situation ensues when those who request data or information want support for a specific point of view or decision. Working out appropriate responses in this atmosphere depends on the role of the office in the institution, how previous situations of this sort were handled, and the directions of the researcher's supervisor. There are no easy answers. Preserving data and information integrity are hallmarks of sound research, but frequently data are incomplete or may be reasonably interpreted in different ways so that support for the desired viewpoint or decision seems to flow from the data.

Effective reporting also requires producing the report in time for it to be useful. This seems like a simplistic admonition, but the timeframe in which a college representative must make a decision or respond to an external question or allegation may not permit implementing the sort of research one would ideally conduct in order to give a comprehensive response. Researchers who fail to produce reports in a timely fashion may quickly find themselves outside the critical information loop of the institution. Exemplary reports delivered after the fact may be useful historical documents, but they erode the value of research to the decision-makers at the institution.

Messages About You

The discussion above is focused on the subject of the report or chart, and the audiences to whom the documents are being directed. There is a different and equally important set of factors, however, that should be taken into consideration when preparing materials. These relate to messages the report will convey implicitly, and are captured in the question "What messages about my institution, my office, or me do I want this work to convey?"

In the 1940s, Dale developed a "cone of experience" depicting how people learn (see Dale, 1969). Dale asserts that people generally remember "10% of what we read, 20% of what we hear, 30% of what we see, 50% of what we see and hear, 70% of what we discuss with others, 80% of what we experience personally, and 95% of what we teach someone else." Following his logic, at least half of what is learned is delivered through a combination of visual image and audio communication. Dale's concept emphasizes the importance of paying attention to the appearances of everything, not only written and presentation materials, but even of ourselves. It also suggests the importance of voice tone, inflections, speed, and word choices in oral presentations, whether these are formal or informal. In addition, Dale's concept suggests that long narratives and tables with many numbers are less likely to have impact and be recalled, let alone used, than shorter written reports and oral presentations. Short reports may refer to longer, technical documents for those interested in pursuing more detail.

Topics such as presenting oneself and one's office are not typically given a great deal of attention by institutional researchers, but they are critical components of effective reporting. Proficient, high quality presentations of self and office enhance the salience, utility, and credibility of reports. Conversely, unprofessional presentations invite audiences to question the quality and contents of reports themselves and the ability of researchers to conduct credible or useful studies for or about the institution.

The discussion in this chapter may seem rudimentary; however, researchers may well forget to spend time considering their client and audiences, especially when they routinely replicate a report every semester or year, or when the complexities of implementing research obscure the original purposes for the project. Thus, it does no harm to be reminded of the importance of client and audiences. Now, having considered how a report's client and audiences affect reporting, we turn to reports themselves.

Chapter 3
Reports

Reports about higher education institutions are written for a number of purposes and can be classified into types, based on content and overall purpose. In this chapter various report purposes and types of reports are described. The typology is based largely on the work of Seybert (1994). Though the types are discussed as unique, it should be evident that a given document might fall into several classifications.

Purposes of Reports

As noted in the preceding chapter, the primary purpose of a report or presentation is to communicate information to meet clients' and audiences' needs. These needs will have been established during the process of determining the client, purpose, and audiences for the report. While each report or presentation will have its unique purpose, in general, reports are designed either to inform the audience, persuade the audience, or both. Subsumed under these general designations, five specific purposes for reports stand out. Reports might contain analyses and interpretations of data and information, or simply compilations of data. The five specific purposes are:

1. Historical record. Some reports, e.g., factbooks, are produced for historical, archival purposes as much as for current use.

2. Support for planning or decision making. Reports may be designed to provide data and information to support either current or future decisions.

3. Public relations. Some reports are produced for the primary purpose of putting the institution into a good light and directly or indirectly influencing readers to have a positive opinion. Economic impact studies are a good example of public relations reports.

4. Information dissemination. Occasionally reports are produced simply to disseminate information. These may be requested by a client or initiated by the institutional research office.

5. Compliance with external reporting requirements. Some reports are produced to meet state governing board, legislative, or accreditation agency mandates.

Types of Reports

- **Survey or major project reports** are usually fairly inclusive documents that present descriptions of methodology, comprehensive findings, conclusions, implications and recommendations, as well as supporting materials. Such reports are likely to have multiple audiences at different levels of authority and responsibility in the institution and with different special areas of interest. When a report is especially long, it might be broken into two documents: the report itself, and a technical document or separate appendix that includes detailed tables for readers who want to examine such features as frequency counts and cross-tabulations of multiple variables or subgroups.

- **Projections** provide anticipated information over time about topics such as enrollment, revenues and expenditures, and facilities requirements. In higher education, projections are usually based on a fiscal or academic year. Projections should include data for at least the current year if not several previous years in order to give the reader a benchmark from which to interpret projections. Projections must also include a description of data sources and calculation algorithms. Where possible (and when individuals are willing to make these known), comparisons of previous projections and actual numbers give useful information to enhance interpretations and to reflect typical margins of error between projections and actual results.

- **Accreditation self-studies** are prepared as part of regional accreditation agency requirements for institutional accreditation, or to meet specifications of specialized accrediting bodies that accredit individual programs or unique types of institutions. Accreditation self-studies usually are crafted to conform to standards, conventions, and reporting features established by the accrediting body. Accrediting agencies are beginning to experiment with new approaches to self-studies; for example, the North Central Association and Southern Association of Colleges and Schools permit selected institutions to write special emphasis self-studies that concentrate on one or a handful of topics. If an institution does undertake a non-traditional accreditation self-study, it is most important to clarify the accreditation agency's expectations about what the written report should contain, and how the role of the team visiting the institution might change as a result of the non-traditional self-study. Evaluators and accreditation agency staff members may be unfamiliar with the non-traditional approach and be tempted to apply both traditional and non-traditional standards to the report and visit. Indeed, the more the self-study departs from accrediting agency norms, the more frequent consultation with the agency should be throughout the process to ensure the novel approach does not jeopardize or unduly complicate the institution's accreditation review.

- **Program review and evaluation reports** range from simple summaries focused exclusively on program strengths, to politically sensitive in-depth studies that can affect a program's very existence. Program reviews and evaluations may be shaped by requirements or expectations of external agencies, or internal committees that formulate institutional outlines or standards for such reports. Important components of reports such as these include the clear delineation of who wrote the report, whether it was developed for external or internal purposes or both, and data and information sources on which evaluative statements are based. In the climate of accountability so prevalent in higher education in the nineties, statements of excellence based on perceptions of those within a department or self-reports absent documentation are insufficient for meeting accountability and assessment expectations. Rather, patterns of evidence must be provided to substantiate summary or evaluative conclusions.

- **Factbooks** are hard copy or electronic compilations of basic institutional data about programs offered, enrollments, costs to students, library and other resources, faculty, residence hall accommodations, intercollegiate athletics, and so forth. Often revised annually, factbooks serve as quick references. Data from other factbooks are often used by peer institutions when conducting peer comparisons. Recently many institutions have begun making their factbooks available electronically on the World Wide Web (WWW), sometimes discontinuing the production of hard copies entirely. Whenever possible, data in factbooks should be consistent with data reported elsewhere, such as in Integrated Postsecondary Education Data System (IPEDS), state agency reports, or accreditation studies. This approach not only reduces or eliminates

16

the need to tabulate similar information by different calculations, but also eliminates questions about why what appears to be the same information—for example enrollment is different in multiple reports that reflect the same data or information.

- **Planning reports** range from comprehensive strategic plans intended to set an institution's course over the next five to ten years to shorter-term program-specific plans that identify measurable objectives to be accomplished over the coming year or two. Planning reports themselves might not contain a great deal of quantitative data, but high quality planning is dependent on data and information. Companion technical reports or appendices providing detailed data and information may supplement short planning reports themselves. Often these technical reports include data about trends though to affect the institution, such as changes in the demography of a college's service area, or in the number and nature of competitor's seeking to recruit from the same pool of potential students.

- **Technical reports and memoranda** usually focus on a narrow subject, and are developed for a small audience that has a direct interest in the subject. The audience for these documents may be more willing to move through detailed data because of their inherent interest in the subject. However, they may not be familiar with relevant variables or data, and therefore may need thorough definitions and explanations.

- **Financial reports** include general annual reports, cost per credit hour or full-time equivalent (FTE) reports, program revenue/cost studies, and budget presentations, among others. Depending on the audience for the report, it may be useful to incorporate basic definitions to help the reader understand concepts that are unfamiliar outside the educational community. Even if the audience is familiar with variables, it is important to include information about how the variables are derived. For example, is the FTE student count based on a denominator of 12 or 15 credit hours for the semester or a denominator of 24 or 30 for the academic year?

- **Peer group comparisons** are reports that present the institution's data about topics such as faculty salaries or workload and comparable data from peer institutions, either as a group or school-by-school. Providing the names of institutions in the peer group is very important so the reader can identify with whom the specific college or university is being compared. Researchers may find that identifying the relevant peer group is a research project itself. There may be different peer groups for different purposes; for example, a peer group for faculty recruitment and salaries, a different peer group for student recruitment, and yet a third peer group for athletics. Sometimes peer groups are identified based on documented comparability on relevant variables, sometimes they are determined by governing boards or associations, and sometimes they are determined by college officers who aspire to be associated with a particular set of institutions. It is important to provide explanatory notes to indicate where costs or revenues labeled identically are calculated by different algorithms. For example, credit hours are calculated typically on semester or quarter credits, but comparing credit hours for a group of schools, some on the quarter system and some on the semester system, requires either calibrating credits to one metric, such as semesters, or adding a clarifying note to indicate which institutions use quarter and which use semester hour credits. The ongoing University of Delaware National Study of Instructional Costs and Productivity (Middaugh, 1999) is an example of a peer group comparison effort.

- **Market analyses** are studies that focus outside the institution itself. They provide information that can affect what occurs internally or suggest ways in which the institution itself can affect the external world in which it operates. Market analyses force the institution to place itself in a broader context, to examine many elements that are beyond the control of the college or university. Six examples of market analyses are: needs assessments, labor market studies, environmental scanning reports, enrollment management studies, economic impact studies, and community image/perception assessments.

1. Needs assessments are explorations that help determine what types of educational programs, courses, and services various populations in the institution's service area might need, with the emphasis normally being on the skill and knowledge domains in which they are currently deficient. As Aslanian and Brickell (1980) point out, however, it is probably more useful to consider

18

demand rather than need alone as a more powerful determinant of potential enrollment. They define demand as comprising three elements: need, motivation, and resources. Need means the person has a reason for acquiring knowledge or skills, perhaps to meet employer expectations, to prepare for a new job, or to overcome a deficiency that impedes job or personal advancement. Motivation means the person is stirred to take action; it does not matter whether motivation is prompted by some external influence such as an employer or the individual's personal desires. Resources include money, time, and the ability to access the educational experience. With the explosion of distance education, resource requirements are rapidly changing, with many new options available for students who previously had to drive to a fixed site at a specific time to take a course. Aslanian and Brickell's most critical message is that need alone, however great, is unlikely to spur people to participate in higher education if they lack motivation and resources.

Faculty and administrators at institutions that draw from a well-defined, relatively small geographic area, such as community colleges, sometimes request community needs assessments. They do so because they believe discrete education and training needs can be discerned, courses and programs developed to meet those needs, and new students enrolled in these courses and programs. While some useful information can be gained from broad assessments of this sort, their real value lies more in the public relations benefit that results from reaching out to the community, than from the validity and utility of results. Rarely would an institution be able to identify whole new areas of interest that conform to the college's mission and are likely to draw students to programs. Needs assessments conducted in conjunction with specific programs and employers in the field are more likely to produce useful findings, particularly if participating employers encourage or require their employees to enroll in courses or programs shaped to respond to the identified needs, and if potential students have the motivation and resources to participate.

2. Environmental scanning reports examine external trends or incidents that affect or might affect the institution. They range

from brief nuggets of information about some particular trend or incident, such as significant hiring or downsizing of a major employer in the college's area, to sweeping examinations of future trends that can have long-term, profound impacts on the institution. Environmental scanning reports link the institution to its outside environment and should promote the understanding that no college can operate in isolation from its context; rather, the context partially defines opportunities on which the institution may capitalize and challenges with which it must cope.

3. Enrollment management reports usually focus on target populations that comprise the bulk of students at an institution or from which the college wishes to recruit more students. Populations may be defined geographically, by ethnic/racial make-up, by academic achievement, or by age, gender or other demographic characteristics. Enrollment management reports often trace student cohorts through the stages of inquiry, application, acceptance and enrollment, permitting admissions offices to pinpoint critical phases of the process for given subgroups, as well as summaries such as total numbers of applicants, admitted and enrolled students.

4. Community image/perception studies seek to measure the extent to which significant constituent groups outside the college know about and have positive or negative perceptions of the institution. Studies of this type are particularly important where the institution wishes to attract more students from a specific geographical area or subgroup. They are useful for institutions that rely in part on local or state taxes and wish to assess public opinion that could affect tax rates, budgetary authorizations, or decisions to go forward with bond or tax increase referenda. Finally, community image/perception studies can help an institution determine ways to sustain or improve community relationships.

5. Economic impact studies estimate the extent to which the institution contributes to the local economy and labor market through measures such as payroll amounts and proportion of earnings spent locally, whether faculty and staff would be likely to live in the area if they were not employed by the institution,

amount of money spent locally for the purchase of goods and services, and amount of money students spend at local businesses. Standard economic multipliers are used to estimate the extent to which additional business volume is generated by direct institutional, employee, and student expenditures.

There are a number of excellent models for conducting economic impact studies (for example, Johnson, 1994; MacFarland & Yates, 1997; and Sinclair Community College, 1998). Several factors should be considered in deciding whether to conduct these studies. One is the nature of the geographical area served by the institution. If a college is located in a relatively isolated geographical area, reasonable assumptions may be made that many faculty, staff, and perhaps even students, would not be in the community if they were not associated with the institution. Reasonable assumptions may also be made that they are buying most of their goods and services locally, and the institution itself may be making many local purchases, as well. However, if a college is located in a major metropolitan area, such assumptions may be less valid, particularly if the student population is largely commuter and the support staff have other options for employment. It is more difficult to argue that the institution itself is contributing to the local economy if most individuals would be living and working in the community, even if the institution were not present. A second factor to consider is the extent to which national changes in the way business is conducted erode the validity of assertions about institutional contributions to the local economy. For example, bank mergers are rapidly eliminating local banks, national companies and Web-based purchasing programs are eliminating locally-owned vendors. A third factor to consider is the benefit of economic impact studies, even if assertions about the institution's contribution to the local economy are somewhat muted. The institution is still contributing to the larger economy, whether in a metropolitan region, a state, or the nation. Using even the most conservative multipliers and excluding financial transactions that are somewhat marginal (spending in hotels and restaurants by parents attending orientation or parent week-ends, for example), most economic impact studies demonstrate a substantial economic impact.

21

Report components

In the following section, a comprehensive list of components that may be included in a report is provided. The report's purpose, audience, and complexity will affect choices about which components to include. For example, a meaningful title is always important, but a list of references may not be relevant and a table of contents might seem pretentious.

1. **Meaningful title.** Often the title alone must convince the audience to read the report. When reports are intended for distribution to a wide, external audience, including other institutional researchers and the scholarly community, the report title needs to include key words or phrases that will serve to identify the report through the Education Resource Information Center (ERIC) and other search processes. The title can be part of a complete title page or report cover that provides the name, mail addresses (including e-mail and Web site), and telephone numbers of the author(s) or office issuing the report.

2. **Executive summary**. No more than one to two pages, the executive summary provides a very brief description of the methodology, results, and implications of the study. The executive summary is intended to stand alone from the report as well as to be a first section within a more comprehensive document. Consequently, the executive summary needs to be tightly written, present only the most meaningful elements of the research design and significant numerical data, highlight overall conclusions and implications, and tell the reader where to obtain the full report or more information.

3. **Table of contents.** As important as the report title, the listings within the table of contents should give clear information about what is contained within each section or presented in each table or figure. Including a table of contents also serves as a reminder to number report pages, a simple procedure that is too often neglected.

4. **Introduction and purpose**. The introduction and purpose describe the purpose of the study, including who requested it and why. Reports that are generated annually should contain a sentence or two indicating this fact. Reports that present results from part of a larger project should contain a brief description of the more comprehensive project and, if possible, a reference to where results from other components of the project can be found. The

introduction might also include a list of those who performed the study, or at least the college office that did so, and members of committees that were involved if the report reflects either the work of a committee or if the project was undertaken at the request of a committee. Though not typically a part of research reports, acknowledgments to colleagues, staff members, and student employees who played a role in the project serve as a permanent thank you to them as well as a reminder to others that projects often rely on cooperative efforts from a number of individuals.

5. **Methodology.** Almost any project relies on a methodology for data collection and analysis, even if this is an informal review of the literature or scattered conversations and anecdotal evidence. The methodology needs to be explained. However, where the methodology is particularly technical or complex, the report narrative itself should be relatively brief, with more comprehensive explanations provided in an appendix. If the research was based on sample data, the methodology section should also include a description of the sampling methodology, characteristics of the sample, and if available, comparisons of relevant variables between the sample, and the full population.

6. **Findings.** For many readers, the findings, along with conclusions, implications, and recommendations, will comprise the heart of a report. Often findings can be presented both in narrative and tabular/graphic forms. Particularly detailed tables should be placed in appendices so as not to unduly interrupt the flow of the report. Where findings are fairly extensive, it will be especially helpful to readers to subdivide the findings into sections.

7. **Summary, conclusions, implications, and recommendations.** These are described as one section, although in particularly long reports they might be divided into separate subsections. The conclusion and/or summary presents a concise review of the primary findings. Implications and recommendations are more action-oriented and may not be appropriate if the subject of the report is presentation of data and information alone, rather than linkage with policy or practice. Even where there are policy or practical linkages, it may be outside the assignment or level of comfort for report writers to make recommendations. The politics

and culture of an institution, as much as the competencies of the researchers will affect whether or not recommendations should be incorporated into a report.

8. **References.**   A list of references is essential when a report cites the literature or internal institutional reports, documents or interviews. A reference list is useful, as well, to cite similar works that shaped or influenced the project. Provision of a list of references enhances the credibility of the report even if the references are not directly cited in the report. Faculty experts in the subject area can be asked to suggest key references on the topic and to indicate what resources might be viewed as suspect by the scholarly community. The process of consulting with faculty can serve as a vehicle for building trust between researchers and faculty and build a foundation for subsequent projects, as well. If researchers conduct numerous studies about a particular topic, it may be useful to create a list of references for each topic and to update it as new literature appears. Then it becomes a simple task to include a list of references in a report, or a note indicating a list of references is available upon request.

9. **Glossary.** Glossaries define acronyms or technical terms and present material that would otherwise lengthen the major narrative component of a report. They are particularly useful in long documents intended for audiences that may not be familiar with acronyms or technical terms. Though part and parcel of the vocabulary of most institutional researchers, acronyms such as IPEDS, SRK, GRS, and SOICC[3] are hardly familiar to most audiences for higher education reports. Indeed, the first time an acronym is used, it should be written out, with the acronym in parentheses. The glossary is a separate section that can be found easily and referred to repeatedly by readers of the report. Once provided in a glossary, definitions or explanations of acronyms rarely have to be repeated within the main body of the document.

10. **Appendices, exhibits, attachments.** These materials appear at the end of a report. They furnish more detailed information and illustrations than are needed in the body of the report. They may include copies of surveys or other instruments used for data collection, tabular displays of detailed data, lists of project

participants or participating groups, scripts for telephone or in-person interviews, copies of memoranda or letters or other relevant communications, or copies of relevant sections of laws or regulations affecting the topic of the report. Terabian (1992) defines an appendix as a group of related items that is too long to be incorporated in the body of a report and is always placed at the end. Materials of different categories should be placed in separate appendices, with each appendix given a distinct number or letter as well as a descriptive title. The American Psychological Association (APA)(1994) style uses letters rather than numbers for each appendix.

Report Readability

Determining the reading level of a report is something about which researchers are rarely concerned. However, tailoring the reading level to the audience can improve the effectiveness and utility of the report and, therefore, its overall value. According to Fink (1995), most people are comfortable reading at a level slightly below their ability. A number of readability tests are incorporated in word processing software programs. Word 6.0 automatically calculated the readability of this paragraph. For example, The Flesch Reading Ease test computs readability based on the average number of syllables per word and the average number of words per sentence. Scores range on the test from 0 (zero) to 100. Standard writing averages approximately 60 to 70; the higher the score, the greater the number of people who can readily understand the document. The Flesch-Kincaid Grade Level test computes readability based on the average number of syllables per word and the average number of words per sentence. The score indicates a grade-school level; for example, a score of 10.0 means a well-prepared tenth grader would understand the document. Standard writing for a lay audience approximately equates to the seventh-to-eighth grade level. The Coleman-Liau Grade Level test uses word length in characters and sentence length in words to determine a grade level, while the Bormuth Grade Level test uses word length in characters and sentence length in words to determine a grade level.

Readability tests included in Word 6.0 produced the following results regarding the paragraph above: Flesch Reading Ease - 48; Flesch-Kincaid Grade Level - 10.3; Coleman-Liau Grade Level - 13.3; Bormuth Grade Level - 10.6. These findings suggest that the reading level of the paragraph is appropriate for an audience that reads at the junior-senior level of high school, so the paragraph should be appropriate for a college-educated audience.

General Comments on Reports with Quantitative Data

Writing effective reports featuring quantitative data requires careful balance between presenting "the numbers" and overwhelming the audience. Even straightforward data, such as tabulations and averages, may frustrate readers who lack the time or the interest to scrutinize long tables of tiny print. Reports that present statistical analyses are even more formidable, both to write and to read. Researchers comfortable with numeric symbols and algebraic formulas may not recognize the extent to which such material may discourage audiences from reading a report.

What are some strategies for improving the effectiveness of reports that convey primarily quantitative data for lay audiences? One is to summarize key findings in both narrative and numeric forms. This technique permits readers who rely on text and those who rely more on numbers to both have access to the material, it also serves to increase the likelihood of findings being remembered because they are repeated, albeit in different formats. A second strategy is to recognize that statistical significance may not have substantive significance for decision makers, a point made well by Astin (1991). Even if one feels compelled to note statistical significance in the report, including a simple description of what is meant by statistical significance will be helpful. Third, judiciously insert tables and graphics within the body of the report; as noted above, one may put long tables in appendices or even in supplementary technical reports that have a more limited distribution. Fourth, whenever a statistical analysis is used, such as chi-square or multiple regression, provide a brief narrative description of what that analysis demonstrates. Fifth, consider presenting the report in a question-answer format, rather than as a holistic narrative or series of tables and charts. Sixth, distribute the findings in one-page briefs and/or Web pages, referring readers to the full report if they are interested. Seventh, include anecdotes and quotations to enliven the report and add a personal dimension. Finally, periodically ask representatives of your audience to talk about ways to improve reports.

Recently Bers worked with a faculty member who, in turn, asked a group of her colleagues to critique several major reports prepared annually by the Office of Research. Faculty stated clearly that they wanted to know what the research findings said about students and how they could use the findings. They were far less interested in what they considered to be the more technical aspects of the research, such as the extent to which the sample of respondents mirrored the entire student population in terms of demographic and educational characteristics. This feedback prompted the department to reorganize subsequent reports to move substantive findings to the front, and to make greater use of appendices and companion technical reports for describing research processes and sample and population characteristics.

Focus Group Reports

Focus group research appears to be growing in popularity among those doing research in and about higher education. While there are a number of excellent books and articles describing focus group research, few contain much information about focus group reports. This section includes a description of alternative formats for reporting focus group results, suggests language to convey recommendations or important concepts, and provides some general observations about focus group reports.

All reports should include certain basic information about the focus group project, including its purpose, a general description of participants, and findings. Depending on the type of report, time, and resources available, and the level of formality of the desired document, other sections may be added. These can include descriptions or actual documents, such as the discussion guide used by the moderator, criteria and screening of eligible participants, setting in which the group was conducted, verbatim quotations to support findings, interpretation of the results, recommendations for action, and an evaluation of the project.

As might be gleaned already from the preceding paragraph, there are many versions of focus group reports, ranging from virtually no report at all — perhaps a simple memorandum summarizing the basic information noted above, to a lengthy report that includes pages of verbatim quotations from the participants. Goldman and McDonald (1987), Templeton (1994), Krueger (1994), and Krueger (1998) present the most complete discussions in the literature about focus group reports.

Goldman and McDonald caution that the ideal qualitative report, and focus group research is qualitative research, lies somewhere between "good science and good journalism" (p. 171). Reports are not sequential summaries or transcripts of the group discussion. Krueger (1994) suggests three ways to present findings. The first is to present a question or idea followed by all participant comments. It is probably the least useful report because it becomes tedious to read and contains little or no interpretive analysis. The second type is a summary description, which contains a concise summary of what participants said about a topic or question followed by illustrative quotations. The third is interpretive. This report builds on the descriptive summary by including interpretations about what the findings mean and what they imply for action or decision-making.

In a more recent work, Krueger (1998) presents four styles of focus group reports: narratives, report memos, top-line reports, and bulleted reports.

- **Narrative or Full Reports.** According to Templeton (1994), the narrative is the longest, most complex, most expensive written report, and usually contains verbatim quotations to illustrate findings and to support interpretations and recommendations. Templeton says full reports can be viewed in two ways. First, they can be viewed as prepared documents that proceed from the statement of a problem to recommendations for its resolution. Second, they can be viewed as a process. The moderator/report writer "converts the often tangled or ambiguous verbal and behavioral amalgam recorded on tapes — plus any written reactions — into a systematic summary of what (in the researcher's judgment) the data meant: what was conveyed and intended, and the ways this intelligence can be used to achieve the desired results" (p. 32).

  The full report contains a table of contents; executive summary; statement of the problem being examined (background and purpose of the project); the methods and procedures used, including major discussion areas and questions; description of the participants; findings, which might include implications and recommendations; and appendices. In some projects, implications or recommendations or both might be outside the scope of the project, at least for formal presentation in the report. Appendices include items such as screening instruments, moderator guides, detailed descriptions of participants, materials used as prompts/props, and verbatim quotes in addition to those incorporated in the findings sections.

  The findings section usually includes subsections. Templeton suggests four subsections. The first is what she calls the interactive climate, brief sketches of facets of group activity that bear on the interpretation of participant reactions. The second subsection is about predispositions, or the attitudes, prior experiences, feelings, prejudices, and habits through which participants are likely to filter communications and decide how to behave with regard to the program or institution or product. The third subsection describes participants' reactions to materials they may have been asked to review during the focus group, for example, college publications. The last subsection is a summary of the findings, a synthesis of the preceding subsections, and implications or recommendations that arise from the findings. Not all reports will include implications or recommendations. Sometimes the report writer will not be in a position to offer even the most tentative statements about implications or recommendations; sometimes findings will be so vague or contradictory that the researcher is reluctant to present them with more clarity than is their due.

- **Report Memos.** The second type of report Krueger noted in 1998 is the report memo. This is a brief summary of key findings, only one to two pages long. The target audience is composed of those who participated in the focus groups themselves. Krueger suggests that the memo include a thank you to participants, a brief summary of key findings, recommendations, and a description of what is currently happening or is planned to implement the recommendations.

- **Top-line Reports.** The top-line report is the most economical. It is relatively brief, spotlights the report writer's interpretations of findings without providing back-up rationale or quotations from the session, is relatively inexpensive and quick to prepare, and tends to have a breezy tone. Top-line report formats are very flexible and frequently adequate to convey the essential nature and results of the project. Krueger says the top-line report is often confused with the executive summary from a narrative report, but they are quite different. The latter highlights critical points from a full report, whereas a top-line report provides quick feedback. Careful analysis may not be done at all when a top-line report is prepared, or the report itself may not provide the analysis.

- **Bulleted Reports.** Like top-line reports, bulleted reports are short and prepared for rapid feedback. Carefully chosen phrases and words are used to convey concepts. Bulleted reports may be all that is required in the way of reporting, but by definition they lack the richness and comprehensiveness of more complete reports. Bulleted reports may serve as excellent handouts to accompany an oral presentation or as an appendix to a full or narrative report, particularly if recipients of the longer document have additional audiences to whom they wish to provide a succinct description of the study.

Those who write focus group reports often struggle with the appropriateness or choice of language to convey findings and recommendations. One of the most common struggles relates to presenting quantitative values. Words like "typically," "commonly," and "infrequently" suggest frequency without being specific as to the consensus or the proportion of focus group participants who shared a particular view. Such words are appropriate for focus group reports, while terms like "50% of the participants" are not.

Focus group report writers may want to make recommendations but find themselves cautious about doing so. Goldman and McDonald (1987) suggest phrases that reflect caution yet permit the writer to offer recommendations. Adapted for higher education, examples are:

"The qualitative findings give reason for optimism about potential student interest in a degree in..."

"Results of this study suggest that viewbook version #3 is most promising because it elicited more enthusiastic reaction and answers questions young students ask about a college..."

Another issue with which focus group report writers struggle is the extent to which verbatim quotations should be incorporated in the document. A narrative, full report clearly has more space and offers more latitude for incorporating verbatim quotations than do top-line or bulleted summary reports. Quotes should be selected judiciously, to illustrate key points rather than to present resounding evidence in support of a particular finding or interpretation. Quotes can also be useful to illustrate the language actually used by participants. They are especially helpful when the purpose of the focus group is to glean wordings on ideas for promotional campaigns or informational materials, or to word research instruments that will be distributed to a larger audience from whom participants are drawn. Including a few particularly trenchant or colorful quotes can enliven a report, but having to wade through pages of quotations will rarely be appreciated by readers.

Finally, a focus group report should not reduce project results to tables with numerical summaries of findings. This approach may save paper and be a stalwart attempt to condense information into a readily accessible format, but is improper because it implies quantitative, generalizable data that focus groups do not provide.

As should be evident from this chapter, producing effective reports requires not only good writing or speaking skills, but understanding and sensitivity to features such as a report's client, audiences, purpose, and structure. Clearly, a single report is rarely suitable for multiple uses, but institutional researchers rarely consider or take the time to prepare different versions of the same research project. Improving the effectiveness of reporting may require this approach, however. It might be useful for institutional researchers to experiment, taking a single research project and purposefully crafting multiple reports using different reporting styles. Testing each style with multiple audiences can be enlightening, productive, and can give concrete evidence for preferred report styles and the level of each style's effectiveness for different audiences.

Chapter 4
Mind, Messages, and Eyes and Brains

Several basic concepts and principles about how human beings perceive, process, and interact with visual materials provide important guidelines for creating high quality reports and displays. This chapter presents some essential information as a framework and vehicle for expanding knowledge about these complex phenomena, along with some general ideas for using design elements that are too often taken for granted.

Communication and Meaning

Meggs (1989) notes that every graphic form or chart is both an optical phenomenon with visual properties and a communicative signal that, with other signals, forms a message. The communicative role occurs within a culture; transmitting information entails the use of a predetermined system or code understood by those within the culture. The cultural framework within which communication takes place is rarely thought about by institutional researchers, but taking some time to think about the culture of the broader society, as well as the specific organization or community, or department that comprises the audience for the report can be a useful approach to articulating and improving reporting.

Communication takes place within a system that has distinct components (Shannon & Weaver, 1949). The information source produces the message or raw information that is to be transmitted. The transmitter or encoder transforms the information into a signal that is suitable for the channel of conveyance. The channel itself is the vehicle along which the signal is transmitted. The receiver or decoder translates the signal back into the original message or an approximation of it. Finally, the recipient or destination receives the decoded message.

Each culture has a set of shared signs and experiences that convey messages, and within cultures each individual has a personal world shaped by his or her unique experiences and learning. The individual's world includes a perceptual filter that serves as an often undetected screen, allowing some messages to move through undistorted, blocking some messages altogether, and reshaping others to change their meanings or the interpretations given to them by the recipient. Thus two people may look at the same graphic display and interpret its message and meaning differently.

Messages, including words and symbols, carry two different types of meaning. One is the denotation, or direct meaning. The other, the connotation, is conveyed or suggested in addition to the denotation, and is shaped by culture, experience, and associations. Thus the selection of words and images needs to be driven by intended denotation and connotation to achieve maximum clarity and accuracy. A simple example should suffice. In one recent study of the Florida performance indicators for community colleges the authors referred to "college prep programs." A reviewer of the manuscript did not know what types of programs that phrase referred to and questioned the absence of references to remedial or developmental education as an attribute describing colleges in the study. It may be that the term "college prep" is less laden with connotations of high school level or below than terms such as "remedial education," but using non-traditional terminology makes it all the harder for readers to understand a report.

People's approaches to graphic space are shaped by habit and custom. In Western cultures, the basic orientation to graphic space is based on a sequence of horizontal lines running from the upper left to the lower right hand corner, with the eye taking in a broad diagonal path, but not every line, from the left to right margin. In designing graphic displays, then, one should consider that the reader is likely to scan a page following the pattern of the letter "Z."

Design Principles and Maxims

A number of design principles, used by graphic designers but also relevant to the presentation of textual material and charts of all kinds, can be employed to help the reader or viewer understand the material by emphasizing the relationships or distinctions among components. Meggs (1989) suggests five such principles.

1. Alignment of forms, by lining up edges or centering forms, suggest relationships and connections.

2. Continuation of forms generate eye movement; for example, the point on an arrow will prompt the eye to move beyond the point itself to the next visual element.

3. Locating forms close to each other in graphic space, the principle of proximity, establishes a relationship, while forms separated by an interval of space are perceived to be more distinct from each other.

4. Forms that share the same or similar visual property, such as shape, size, color, tone, texture, or direction, display correspondence and are perceived to have a more meaningful relationship to each other

than forms which do not share any of these properties.

5. Completion occurs when elements have sufficient relationships because of alignment, continuation, proximity, and correspondence so that they are perceived to form a whole or to be complete.

Edward Tufte (1983, 1990, 1997) has written three books filled with examples of the visual depictions of data and information ranging from some of the earliest graphic presentations of data to much more recent works, covering subjects as diverse as Napoleon's march to Moscow, the frequency of repair records for automobiles, and the alleged criminal activities of witnesses for the prosecution that discredited the witnesses and helped lead to the acquittal of John Gotti. There is no need to duplicate Tufte's numerous examples in this monograph. Indeed, many are unlikely to be of immediate, practical value to individuals preparing reports, tables and charts about higher education. However, the key principles and guidelines Tuft presents about data graphics are pertinent.

Tufte's fundamental principle for effective statistical graphics is: "Above all else show the data" (Tufte, 1983, p. 92). To accomplish this, he recommends these additional principles.

1. Maximize ink devoted to the data themselves. In other words, focus on the information being conveyed, and not on elements such as labels, frames, gridlines, ticks, or other symbols.

2. Minimize ink that does not depict the data. This principle is the complement of maximizing data-ink.

3. Minimize redundant presentations of data; for example, there is no need to have column heights depicting size and gridlines with values labeled, and the actual number represented by each column printed above the column.

4. Revise and edit graphics, sometimes numerous times, in order to achieve the above principles.

More recently, Stephen M. Kosslyn presented what he calls three maxims, or psychological insights, that account for what make graphics effective or ineffective. Kosslyn's work is based on extensive empirical research about how humans perceive and interpret images, both physiologically and psychologically. Each of Kosslyn's maxims is an umbrella for a number of more specific principles (1994). His three maxims are:

1. "The mind is not a camera" (p. 3). Rather than passively receiving images, we "actively organize and make sense of the world" (p. 3). We receive visual images through channels, and when several messages are conveyed through the same channels, distinguishing among them is exceedingly difficult. The mind also groups together marks that are located near each other; that suggest a line; that are similar in size, shape or color; that seem to be going in the same direction; and that are enclosed by paired or common elements such as left and right brackets.

2. "The mind judges a book by its cover" (p. 7). We do judge things by their appearance, and there should be compatibility between the property or message being conveyed and the symbols being used to convey it. For example, higher bars should be used to depict "the growth of a substance; red rather than green should be used to depict financial losses.

3. "The spirit is willing, but the mind is weak" (p. 8). Despite our best intentions, most humans can retain no more than four perceptual groups in mind at once. Chunking larger groups into sets of four will help the message receiver retain the information. Readers need as much help as they can be given, and they should not be expected to make large extrapolations or complex interpretations from graphs.

Barker and Ott (1990) point out that graphs — depictions of numerical relationships — usually demonstrate just four points: 1) size - biggest or smallest; 2) how things change over time; 3) what is typical or exceptional; and 4) how one thing predicts [or is related to] another. They are particularly critical of clutter, or what Tufte refers to as "chartjunk."

Barker and Ott (1990) present a clutter ratio, defined as the components needed to display data divided by all the components of a graph, which include grids, frames, titles, labels, and symbols used to represent data. Simply by removing options that are unnecessary or redundant for displaying data, clutter can be minimized. Wurman (1997) says there are five ways in which to organize, and therefore to present, graphical information: by Location, Alphabet, Time, Category, and Hierarchy. He suggests the acronym LATCH as an easy way to remember these (p. 17).

The principles and maxims of graphic design noted above illustrate an important point regarding the differences between charts and narrative reports: charts eliminate redundancy, yet reports often purposefully build redundancy with the use of executive summaries, headings and subheadings, and deliberate repetitions of key statements or findings.

Using Design Principles and Maxims

Material provided in this chapter may seem more theoretical and esoteric than institutional researchers need for preparing effective reports. However, many reports fail to observe the guidelines and are not as effective as they could be. One reason these oversights occur is because those who prepare reports are unfamiliar with or do not take the time to think about the physical and cultural factors that limit and shape what people are literally able to see and understand. A second reason is that computer software makes it seductively easy to create charts and graphs cluttered with extra dimensions, labels, colors, symbols, artwork, and color. Simple charts may be easier to understand and actually do a better job of conveying key information, but they lack the "wow" factor that many audiences have come to expect. Researchers may be fearful that simple visuals will lead to evaluations of their work as being old fashioned.

Finally, the guidelines can be used as benchmarks against which to measure the effectiveness of reports. Converting design maxims into questions can provide a useful template for this purpose. For example, how much ink is being devoted to the information? How much is being devoted to frames, gridlines, ticks, labels, or other symbols? Has redundancy been built into a chart? Should there be? What can be eliminated without degrading the clarity of the presentation? Creating a template of effective reporting questions and using the template as a tool to audit reports can be an efficient and provocative approach for evaluating the effectiveness of reports. It can also be a powerful mechanism for fostering conversations among colleagues about the elements of effective reports, as well as for assessing whether reports they are producing meet expected or desired standards of effectiveness.

From the discussion in this chapter it should be evident that the ways in which individuals perceive and interpret data are mediated by physical and physiological properties of the brain and neurosystem, and by the cultures and traditions within which they were raised. It is not sufficient simply to create reports and graphics that look attractive or appear impressive. Institutional researchers must weave knowledge of how the mind and eye operate into their design and presentation of reports.

Chapter 5
Elements of Visual Presentations

In this chapter a number of ideas and guidelines are presented to enhance visual presentations, including narrative materials, textual materials, charts, and graphs. The successful design and preparation of visual presentations are contingent on numerous factors, including some that may not normally be considered, such as whether or not it is important for the presentation to be truly first-rate, or whether a lesser quality display will suffice for the purpose at hand. Absent unlimited resources, including one's own time, prudent decisions will have to be made between what needs to be done well, and what simply needs to be done.

Among the most compelling and comprehensive books about depicting data through graphics are those written by Tufte (1983, 1990, 1997). However, a useful, shorter book about preparing charts is Kosslyn's *Elements of Graph Design*. Practical and readable, the volume gives clear recommendations, illustrating most with both good and bad examples of each point. This monograph makes no attempt to duplicate Kosslyn's work, but rather draws from the works of many writers, Kosslyn included, to provide a brief discussion and suggestions related to the most common types of visual presentations used in research about higher education.

When to Graph

Graphs are not always necessary or appropriate for conveying messages clearly and concisely. The advent of easy-to-use computer software programs has been accompanied by a proliferation of graphs in many presentations, but these do not necessarily contribute to the quality of the work. Kosslyn (1994) recommends these guidelines for determining when to use graphs:

- Use graphs when the purpose is to illustrate relations among measurements. However, if the goal is to present precise values rather than impressions of differences, then a table or narrative is more appropriate.

- Craft a precise title to help clarify what message or information is being conveyed and the data that will be needed to do so.

- Decide what questions the reader should be able to answer as a result of the graph, and then organize the data so this can be achieved. Kosslyn uses the concept of "relevance" to elaborate on this idea. The data presented should be relevant to answering the question, and no more than the relevant data should be included. This recommendation is similar to Tufte's admonition to avoid redundancies and extraneous data, images, and labels within charts.

- Use concepts and displays that are familiar to the audience for whom the chart is being developed. For example, the use of mortar boards to symbolize graduates is a common technique in graphs for North American audiences; but mortar boards may lack meaning for audiences in the Middle East or Asia.

Fonts

Appropriate fonts, the style of type, significantly affect the readability, appearance, and implied tone of a communication. A number of general considerations guide font selection. Some relate to demonstrated findings regarding the readability of fonts, and others relate to issues of style, art, and design. Considerations about style, art, and design allow for creativity and flexibility — more in the bailiwick of artists and graphic designers than of individuals who produce research reports and charts. At the risk of oversimplification, some key rules or guidelines for selecting fonts and print styles are presented below. They are derived from a variety of sources and are listed in no particular order.

- Use either serif or sans serif typefaces. Serifs are the tiny extenders on the letters; sans serif fonts have no extenders. Times Roman letters have serifs, but the Arial font does not. There is no consistent difference in readability or legibility between serif and sans serif fonts; other elements such as size, spacing, and lightness or darkness of color are more important in influencing readability.

- Use a combination of capital and small letters. All capitals are very difficult to read, especially in long phrases or narrative passages, because the letters share too many features and are not readily discriminable from each other.

- Use *italics* sparingly. Italic letters, like capitals, share many features and are not readily discriminable from each other. Italics may be used effectively to emphasize a word or brief phrase, but should be avoided in long sentences or passages.

- Use <u>underlining</u> sparingly. Once the only real option for most manuscripts because of typewriter limitations, other alternatives such as bold, italic, or shading are now routinely available for emphasizing words or phrases.

- Use **boldface** for emphasis, though be sure the weight contrasts adequately with text.

- Safe fonts with serifs are Times Roman, Bookman, Century Schoolbook, and Garamond. Arial is a good choice for sans serif typefaces. Courier conveys the appearance of having been done on a typewriter and is frequently perceived as being less professional than other fonts. Line printer suggests raw printouts from a computer; its small size makes it difficult to read as well.

- Mix fonts in the same document, but use only two or three styles at most, and be consistent in their use; e.g., use one font for headlines and another for text.

- Salience means text is easier to read because of size, color or other visual properties. Use more salient labels for more general components of a display or major headings within a narrative.

- Choose font sizes based on two considerations, the absolute size of the character and the distance of the reader. Kosslyn (1994) recommends a simple formula for determining font size: divide the height of the characters by the distance from the reader. A ratio of .007 is considered by the U.S. military to be the relationship permitting people to read easily. Although Fink (1995) says that letters on transparencies should be at least 3/8 inch high, or 18-point, this size is still too small for many audiences. Transparencies should be created with 24-point or bigger to ensure they are visible, and in even larger sizes for presentations in large rooms. In any case, do not produce regular tables in 10 or 12 point for use as transparencies. Not only are these unreadable, they will discourage the audience from paying attention. To illustrate: this is 18-point, and this is 24-point.

White Space

White space, that part of a page, slide, or transparency that does not contain printed elements or illustrations, can be a potent design element that substantially improves or degrades the quality and clarity of data and information being presented. This section provides a number of suggestions for capitalizing on white space to enhance presentations and, thereby, to improve both the substantive quality and appearance of messages being conveyed. Much of what follows is derived from Staley and Stopke (1990).

White space serves several functions, including shaping and framing content, separating content, providing balance through contrast, giving the reader or viewer some rest, and communicating certain effects such as the importance of a statement or the fact that a particular section of narrative presents verbatim quotations. Because white space contains no printed images, it contrasts sharply with what is printed.

White space can be used in many ways to focus or enhance design:

- Use it to establish a rhythm for the reader that extends over multiple pages. The rhythm aids comprehension, recognizability of connected or similar messages; it also inhibits eye fatigue.

- Use it to emphasize important information or serve as background for headlines and subheads that allow the reader to skim the text to locate pertinent information.

- Use it to set off and draw attention to important information by surrounding it with more white space than is normally used in that particular document.

- Use it to signal relationships between elements. For example, using more white space above than below a heading or subheading indicates the heading or subheading fits with the text below it and is a break from what is above.

- Use it to convey a sense of style, elegance, cleanliness, and crispness. All these attributes enhance the document's credibility and audience perceptions of the document's quality.

- Finally, use it to promote readability, especially when it is judiciously combined with appropriate choices of font size and style.

All this is not to say that more white space is always better. Rather, it implies that the use of white space should be by decision and not default.

Color

Color has three essential characteristics: saturation, or deepness of the colors; intensity, or amount of light reflected; and hue, which is what is normally called color. Intensity is measured with light meters, but the human eye and brain perceive intensity as brightness. Relationships among colors are based on all three characteristics, and they are relative. That is, how we perceive a color is dependent in part on its relationship with other adjacent or nearby colors. In selecting colors for a chart, it is important to consider all colors being used because the perception of each depends on the others.

The color wheel is the structured arrangement and relationship of hues, ranging in clockwise order—red, orange, yellow, green, blue and violet. Colors opposite each other—red and green, orange and blue, yellow and violet—are most complementary.

The availability of graphics and presentation software that prepare color output and access to economical color printers and duplicators have greatly expanded the use of color in print documents and especially in presentations using transparencies or computer programs. For many audiences, black and white presentations suggest a lack of professionalism and seem old fashioned, even if the content itself is exemplary. Thus the decision to use or not to use color may be an important decision affecting the effectiveness of a report.

Kosslyn (1994) presents several helpful recommendations regarding the use of colors. These recommendations relate less to the aesthetic appearance of a chart than to the ways in which human beings perceive and interpret color. Because this text is in black and white, only a small number of recommendations are presented. Readers should refer to Kosslyn's book or another text about the use of color to see actual examples of the points made.

Several recommendations are particularly important. Avoid using red and blue or red and green in adjacent regions because the eye perceives a wobble, or wavy effect, where the two colors meet. Avoid using blue if the display will be photocopied. Avoid using these color combinations: green, blue, and gray; black, blue, and brown; white, and yellow (Fink, 1995).

Kosslyn (1994) says that adjacent colors should have different brightnesses. Recall that brightness is subjectively interpreted and can be affected by room lighting, so the viewer may be unable to differentiate between colors of similar brightness. The most important content element should be the most visually salient as well; and warmer colors, such as oranges and roses, should be used in the foreground rather than the background.

Color can be used very effectively to emphasize or convey meaning, as long as the use of color is compatible with convention. For example, the color red is associated with debits and monetary losses; conversely, the color green is associated with credits and monetary gains. Imagine the confusion resulting from a chart depicting profits with red ink and losses with green ink. Using different colors to represent differences in amounts can be confusing because there is no conventional or cultural norm associating colors with quantitative differences (profit and loss can be defined as directions, not amounts per se). Instead, deeper saturations and greater intensities for the same hue effectively depict greater amounts. For example, a pie chart could be used to indicate the proportion of the student population for each major racial/ethnic group (size of wedges), with color showing the distribution of financial aid awarded by racial/ethnic group (saturation and intensity of hue, using the deepest green for the group with the highest average amount of financial aid). Color can also be used to group elements; for example, if two pie charts are used, the same color should be used for wedges that represent the same element in both charts.

Pattern

Even more common than the use of color is the use of pattern to differentiate regions on a chart. In selecting patterns, two considerations are most crucial: ensuring that regions are easily distinguishable from each other visually and preventing visual irritation. Kosslyn (1994) again provides theoretical explanations and recommendations to enhance the use of pattern.

Kosslyn (1994) notes an important concept regarding the use of pattern, and other visual elements: visual properties must be discriminable or distinguishable from each other. That is, "two or more marks must differ by a minimal proportion in order to be distinguished from one another; the critical factor is proportion, not the absolute amount" of the property (p. 170). He goes on to present clear, simple guidelines that can be easily adopted. For example, points located at discrete points in a line should be at least twice as thick as the line itself. If more than one line is used on a chart, discrete point symbols used on each line should be highly discriminable from each other in shape and fill. When using lines at different angles to differentiate regions of a chart, as in the wedges of a pie chart, the lines should be at least 30 degrees apart. When using the same line pattern and angle to differentiate regions, the lines should be spaced at a ratio of at least two to one from one region to the next. For example, if the first region has lines spaced 1/16 of an inch apart, the next region should have the lines spaced either 1/8 of an inch apart or 1/32 of an inch apart.

Figures 1 though 3 contain examples of lines, angles, and segments that obscure or facilitate discriminability.   They are from Kosslyn (1994) and are reproduced with permission.

Figure 1
Lines

Source: Stephen M. Kosslyn. *Elements of Graph Design*.
New York: W.H. Freeman and Company, 1994. Used with permission.

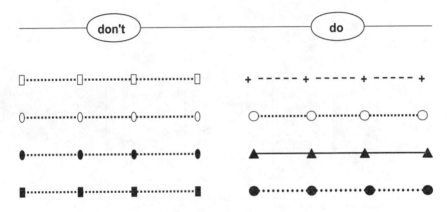

Studies have shown that the four lines and symbols on the right are highly discriminable

Figure 2
Angles and Line Orientation

Source: Stephen M. Kosslyn. *Elements of Graph Design*.
New York: W.H. Freeman and Company, 1994. Used with permission.

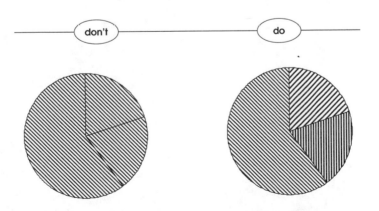

Line orientations must be immediately discriminable to delineate regions clearly

Figure 3
Segments

Source: Stephen M. Kosslyn. *Elements of Graph Design*.
New York: W.H. Freeman and Company, 1994. Used with permission

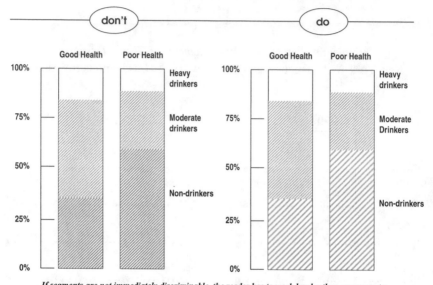

If segments are not immediately discriminable, the reader has to work harder than necessary to compare corresponding elements

Chapter 6
Tables and Charts

The variety of presentations in which tables and charts can appear is infinite. With the advent of software applications that permit easy manipulation of data and the use of graphic illustrations and artwork of all types, constructing elaborate representations of data and information no longer is technically difficult. However, ease of construction has a downside: the tendency to overdo graphic illustrations can make data less clear than simpler designs.

Depictions of data and information, both narrative and graphic, contain a number of elements. The glossary in this book provides a list and brief definitions of elements derived from Kosslyn (1994), Mims (1987), Wallgren et al. (1996), and White (1984). The glossary serves as a reminder about the appropriate contents of charts, a prompt to eliminate elements that unnecessarily clutter charts, and a common language to use with graphic designers to prepare visual materials.

Tables

Tables are perhaps the only way to present exact, detailed data about a large number of variables. Tables can also be extremely effective vehicles for reporting simple information in a visual format that makes the data more accessible to the reader than imbedding the data in a narrative. A key to using tables effectively is to determine whether a great amount of detailed data is needed by the reader, or if simpler graphic displays or summary tables will meet their needs. In making this decision, it is important to consider the fact that while tables are often the only feasible means of portraying exact data, they may demand patience and concentration from the reader. The zeal to convey all data in great detail needs to be tempered by the understanding that many readers have neither the interest nor the tolerance required to read and extract meaning from data presented in dense tables. Moving detailed tables to appendices or technical reports, for example, and keeping summary tables in the body of a report help to balance the competing demands for simplicity and detail.

In this section, some basic rules for presenting tables are presented. Some of these rules apply to presenting charts as well. Because tables are frequently used in higher education reports, and comprise such a fundamental vehicle for expressing data and information, it is important to pay special attention to the rules for tables.

A list is the most basic type of table. When preparing lists, items should be written with parallel structure; for example, begin each point with a verb or repeated phrase such as "Students will..." Items should be of similar length, each placed on a separate line. Numerals should be numbered if they are part of a coherent order or set off by bullets if they are in random order. Indenting the list makes it stand out from the surrounding text. Finally, the list should be introduced by a sentence explaining what the list contains.

The narrative paragraph above can be easily transformed into a list.

Basic rules for preparing a list:
• Write items in same way
• Keep items similar in length
• Place each item on separate line
• Set off lines by numbers or bullets
• Indent list from surrounding text
• Introduce list with phrase explaining contents

Other tables contain two or more factors. Wainer (1992) presents three principles regarding tables, all of which are driven by his basic proposition that tables are meant for communication, not data storage. Wainer's principles are:

1. Order rows and columns in a way that makes sense. Several useful ways of ordering are by size, usually largest first; by a natural order such as time, moving from past to future; and by meaningful grouping, such as academic rank of faculty, from instructor to full professor.

2. Round numbers, to two digits if possible, and certainly to no more than two decimal places. It is preferable not to use decimals at all, except in those cases where decimals differentiate meaningfully among data points or it is conventional to include them. Grade point averages in whole numbers make no sense, for example, but grade point averages carried beyond one or two decimal places are typically too detailed to be useful.

3. Provide summaries of rows and columns, the sum or "all," to give benchmarks for comparison. The content of the "all" depends on the purpose. It may be useful to give a total, a median, or a mean. Setting the "all" apart visually from other elements of the tables through the use of rules or bold typeface further highlights these data and facilitates understanding.

A chief challenge in creating a readable table is to space rows and columns so the reading directions — left to right, and up and down — are in balance. Vertical groups of narrow elements (usually the columns) are easier to discern than horizontal elements; this means gaps between columns should be relatively narrow. To further assist the eye's horizontal movement, extra space between lines should be added, or other visual aids such as horizontal rules, shading, or skipping spaces between every fourth or fifth line, can be employed.

Column headings can be centered if they are approximately the same length and do not extend a great deal beyond the column entries; they should be set at the left-hand edge of the column if lengths differ, and words should be stacked in several lines if the title is much wider than the column entries. Using bold lines across the top and bottom of a table or enclosing the entire table in a box or shaded area serve to define the table space and draw the eye to it. In graphic tables, symbols can be used to replace words such as "yes" or "no." For example, checkmarks or darkened squares can symbolize "yes."

Charts

While there are numerous design variations, charts can be classified into five broad categories. Four follow from Barker and Ott's (1990) four types of information based on quantitative questions: size, change over time, typicality or exceptionality, and relationships or predictive associations that two or more variables have to each other. The fifth category encompasses illustrations of relationships of other sorts: people, space, and processes.

Kosslyn (1994) and Wallgren, et al. (1996) provide excellent descriptions and examples of different types of charts, including discussions of common problems with various charts and ideas for emphasizing or focusing attention to key elements. Although only the most common types of charts used in institutional research are included in this monograph, the works by Kosslyn and Wallgren et al. contain many other examples.

The examples that follow are presented in black and white and were prepared using widely available software, so they represent the kinds of charts that should be very "do-able" by all researchers. The appropriate use of color also enhances the effectiveness of charts and increases visual interest (unfortunately cost considerations made color depictions unfeasible for this publication).

Charts that depict size

1. Pie charts show proportional relationships. To be effective, pie charts should not have more than six slices, unless the key point to convey is fragmentation of the whole into numerous small segments. Separating out a slice or putting one into a bold color emphasizes that segment in a pie chart. Figure 4 presents a simple pie chart depicting financial aid by race/ethnicity.

Figure 4
Pie Chart

Percent Financial Aid Awarded by Race/Ethnicity - 1997

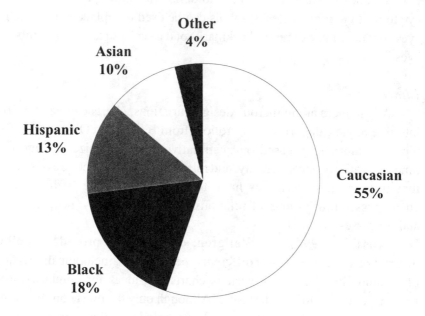

When two or more pie charts are used to depict similar data at two or more points in time or for two or more entities, the same arrangement, color or pattern, label, and separation should be used for each pie. Figure 5 presents two pie charts illustrating these points.

Figure 5
Side by Side Pie Charts

Expenditures by Classification
FY 1998 & FY 1999

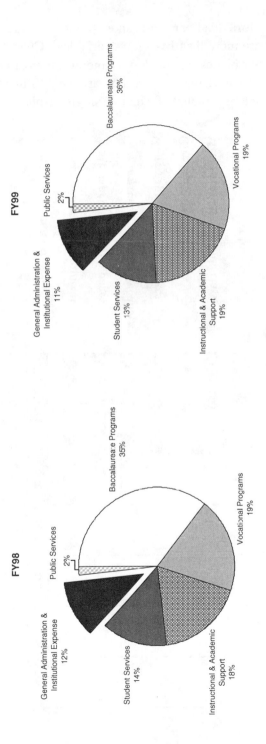

2. Horizontal bar charts show proportional relationships, especially if there are more than five or six variables. Charts should be ordered by size, either biggest or smallest. Among the most compelling features of horizontal bar charts are that they are easy to understand and convey a relatively large amount of data in a single display.

Figure 6
Horizontal Bar

Percent Students Who Engaged in Activity in More Than Half Their Courses

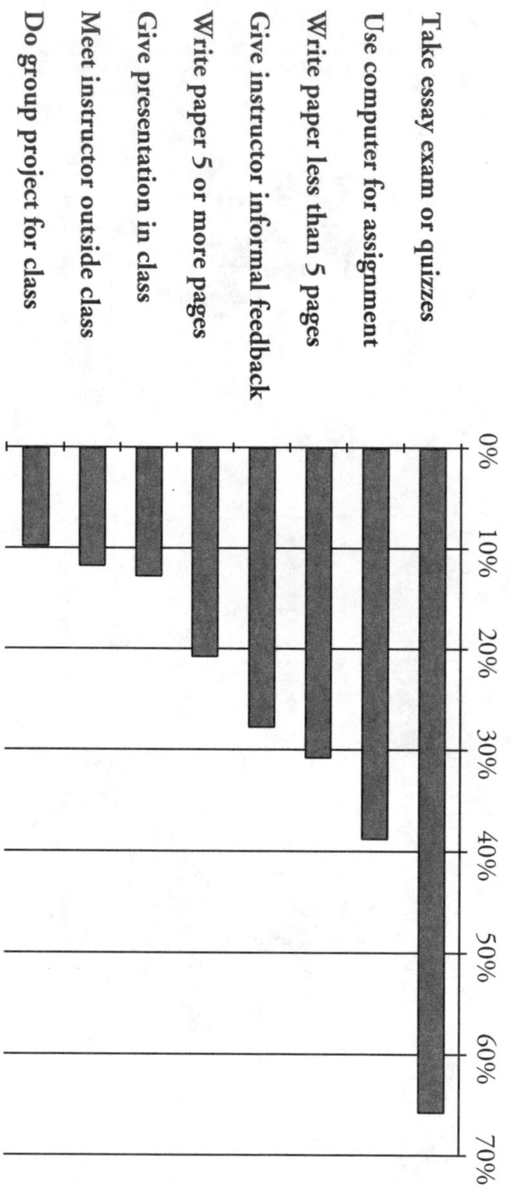

Source: Oakton Current Student Survey, Fall 1997

50

3. Data tables are actually of two types: verbal and graphic. Verbal tables present facts tabulated into words, numbers, or symbols. Higher education researchers are probably most familiar with tables that present a great deal of specific, numerical data. Figure 7 depicts a table with data from the University of Mississippi about the retention of entering freshman classes.

Figure 7
Retention of Entering Freshman Classes
at the University of Mississippi

Retention/Attrition Classification	Entering Freshman Class									
	1987	1988	1989	1990	1991	1992	1993	1994	1995	1996
CUMULATIVE PERCENT RETAINED (GRADUATED)										
After 1 year	76	75	76	77	77	76	74	71	73	75
After 2 years	66	64	63	62	63	63	65	61	62	*
After 3 years	61 (1)	60 (1)	59 (1)	57 (1)	57 (1)	57	62	58	*	*
After 4 years	57 (33)	55 (29)	55 (32)	53 (31)	56 (30)	54 (30)	58 (32)	*	*	*
After 5 years	56 (50)	53 (47)	54 (49)	53 (46)	54 (47)	51 (45)	*	*	*	*
End of 6 years	56 (52)	54 (50)	54 (51)	53 (48)	54 (51)	51 (48)	*	*	*	*
CUMULATIVE PERCENT NOT RETAINED										
After 1 year	24	25	24	23	23	24	26	29	27	25
After 2 years	34	36	37	38	37	37	35	39	38	*
After 3 years	39	40	41	43	43	43	38	42	*	*
After 4 years	43	45	45	47	44	46	42	*	*	*
After 5 years	44	47	46	47	46	49	*	*	*	*
End of 6 years	44	46	46	47	46	49	*	*	*	*
ATTRITION SUBGROUP: CUMULATIVE PERCENT WHO WERE DISMISSAL DROPOUTS										
After 1 year	4	4	4	4	4	5	6	6	5	5
After 2 years	6	7	8	7	6	8	7	8	6	*
After 3 years	8	9	9	7	8	9	8	9	*	*
After 4 years	9	10	9	8	8	10	9	*	*	*
After 5 years	10	10	10	8	9	11	*	*	*	*
End of 6 years	10	9	11	8	9	11	*	*	*	*
ATTRITION SUBGROUP: CUMULATIVE PERCENT WHO WERE VOLUNTARY DROPOUTS										
After 1 year	20	21	20	19	19	19	20	23	22	20
After 2 years	28	29	29	31	31	29	28	31	32	*
After 3 years	31	31	32	36	35	34	30	33	*	*
After 4 years	34	35	36	39	36	36	33	*	*	*
After 5 years	34	37	36	39	37	38	*	*	*	*
End of 6 years	34	37	35	39	37	38	*	*	*	*

*At the time that this table was prepared, sufficient time had not expired for the determination of these percentages.

Graphic tables present a type of tabulation in which criteria are plotted on one axis and locations are plotted on the other (White, 1984). Graphic tables provide visual information that can be quickly interpreted about the presence or absence of some quality. For example, Figure 8 depicts degrees, certificates, and courses available in a number of programs from institutions participating in a higher education consortium serving the northern suburbs of Chicago.

1998-1999 COLLEGE AND UNIVERSITY ACADEMIC PROGRAMS WITHIN THE CONSORTIUM SERVICE AREA

The three regional community colleges also offer associate degree programs in the arts and sciences that parallel the baccalaureate programs on this chart. See the Community College Career Programs chart in this publication.

Legend:
- UC ◆ Undergraduate Courses are offered at the site
- ■ Undergraduate degree is available at the site
- GC ◆ Graduate Courses are offered at the site
- ◆ Graduate degree is available at the site
- X Certificate program

Institution	Mgmt Info Systems	Human Resources Mgmt	Business Administration	Accounting	Business	Theater	Graphic Design	Fashion Design	Fine Arts	Art History
Barat			◆	◆	◆		◆	◆	◆	◆
Columbia Coll of MO			◆							
Concordia			GC	■	GC					
DePaul O-Hare	GC		◆/GC	■	GC					
Dominican										
Elmhurst										
Illinois Institute of Art						◆	◆	◆	◆	◆
Illinois Institute of Technology										
Keller Graduate School	GC	GC	■	GC	GC					
Lake Forest		◆	UC	UC	UC				◆	◆
Lake Forest Graduate School						UC				
Lewis			GC/UC							
Loyola - Wilmette										
National ñ Lewis				UC			UC		UC	
North Central			◆/UC							
North Park University			■							
Northeastern				⬥	⬥					

Figure 8
Graphic Table

Charts that depict change over time

1. Cluster bar charts are especially valuable for grouping multiple variables for easy comparison, such as showing enrollments by ethnic group during a five-year period. An important consideration in creating cluster bar charts is deciding whether to group data for each group or each time period together. Figures 9 and 10 (p. 54) present both options, showing fall enrollments by race/ethnicity during a five-year period. The two approaches emphasize different aspects of the single phenomenon of enrollment by race/ethnicity. The first, which clusters the bars by year, focuses attention on the relative distribution of ethnic groups in the student population. The second, which clusters the bars by race/ethnic group, emphasizes the change in numbers within each group over the five-year period. The question being addressed will determine which approach to use; is the interest in the relative distribution of ethnic groups, or on the change in numbers within each group over time?

Figure 9
Cluster Bar

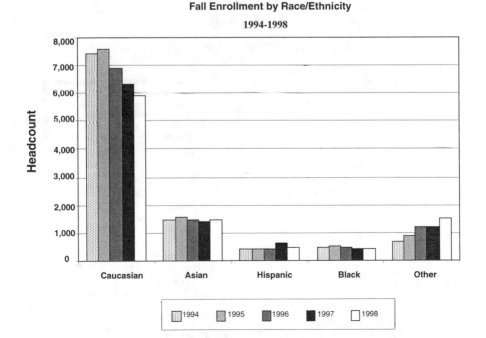

Fall Enrollment by Race/Ethnicity

1994-1998

Figure 10
Cluster Bar

Fall Enrollment by Race/Ethnicity

1994-1998

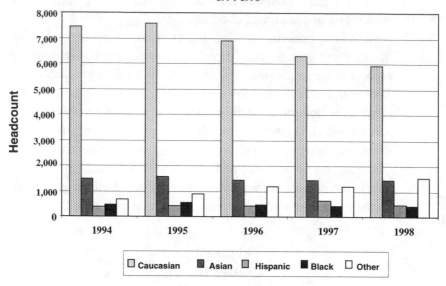

Figure 11
Line Chart

5-Year Institutional Graduation Rates
Public & Private 4-Year Institutions
1983-1997

Graduation rates dropped from
60% to 56% in private schools,
52% to 43% in public schools,
58% to 52% overall.

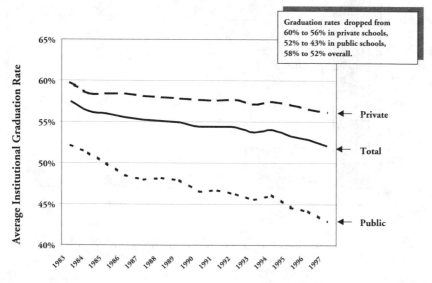

2. Line charts show trends and can be used to display an almost unlimited number of data points. However, no more than five to six lines should be contained on a single graph. Variations in line style and weight help to distinguish one line from another, especially if lines cross or are near each other. Putting labels on or near a line rather than in a separate legend further facilitates understanding. Figure 11 depicts graduation rates from public and private institutions.

3. One hundred percent bar charts display how proportional relationships change during time. They can show numerous proportional relationships in a single chart, but note that changes in totals during time are not reflected, because each bar depicts 100% of whatever the total is. One can easily (and erroneously) assume the total has remained stable if he or she does not immediately grasp that data are represented as percentages of whatever the total happens to be for that year. Figure 12 depicts the percent of applications by race/ethnicity. Figure 13 (p. 56) presents the same data, but for the absolute number rather than the percent of applications; this depiction clearly shows changes in the overall number of applications. Neither chart successfully shows changes in the number of percent of applications for any group except Caucasians.

Figure 12
One Hundred Percent Stacked Bar Chart
Percent of Applications by Race/Ethnicity

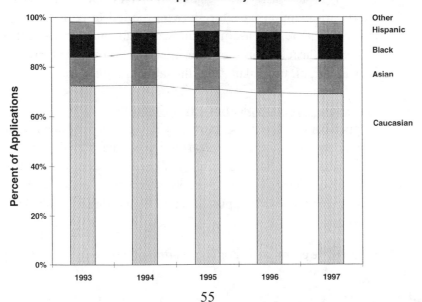

55

Figure 13
Stacked Bar Chart

Total Number of Applications by Race/Ethnicity

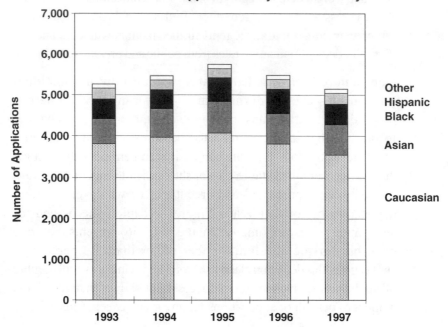

4. Area or surface charts show change in volume during time. These charts are inappropriate for showing period-to-period changes (trends), but are very useful in showing cumulative totals. Figure 14 depicts the retention of one freshman cohort from the University of Mississippi, using data from the table in Figure 7.

Charts that show what is typical or exceptional

1. Stepped bar charts are also known as histograms. The shape of the histogram shows the overall distribution of data, with the height of each bar representing the number of occurrences or observations for each category. Figure 15 (p. 58) shows the number of student visits to Instructional Support Services for tutoring each day during one year.

2. Cumulative charts are bar or line charts that show how things change

Figure 14
Area Chart

University of Mississippi Retention of Entering Freshmen

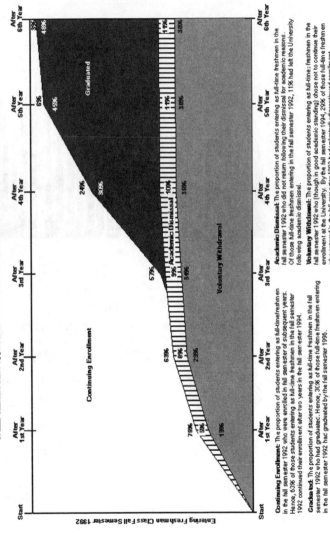

THE UNIVERSITY OF MISSISSIPPI
ENROLLMENT STATUS OF MEMBERS OF ENTERING FRESHMAN CLASS
FALL SEMESTER 1992 AND AT THE END OF EACH OF THE NEXT SIX YEARS

Continuing Enrollment: The proportion of students entering as full-time freshmen in the fall semester 1992 who were enrolled in fall semester of subsequent years. Hence, 63% of those students entering as full-time freshmen in the fall semester 1992 continued their enrollment after two years in the fall semester 1994.

Graduated: The proportion of students entering as full-time freshmen in the fall semester 1992 who had graduated. Hence, 30% of those full-time freshmen entering in the fall semester 1992 had graduated by the fall semester 1996.

Academic Dismissal: The proportion of students entering as full-time freshmen in the fall semester 1992 who did not return following their dismissal for academic reasons. Of those full-time freshmen entering in the fall semester 1992, 11% had left the University following academic dismissal.

Voluntary Withdrawal: The proportion of students entering as full-time freshmen in the fall semester 1992 who (though in good academic standing) chose not to continue their enrollment at the University. By the fall semester 1994, 29% of those full-time freshmen who entered in the fall semester 1992 had voluntarily discontinued enrollment.

Figure 15
Histogram

Instructional Support Services
Student Visits for Tutoring by Day
Academic Year 1997-98

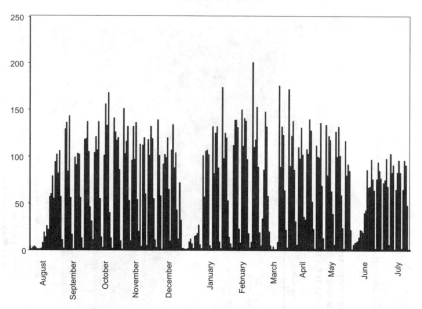

Figure 16
Cumulative Area Chart
Instructional Support Services
Cumulative Student Visits for Tutoring
Academic Year 1997-98

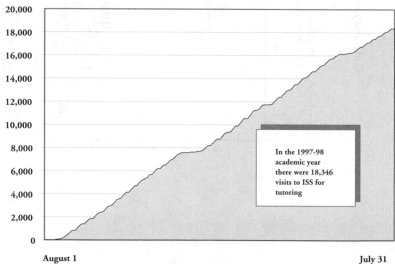

In the 1997-98 academic year there were 18,346 visits to ISS for tutoring

August 1

July 31

over time by presenting cumulative or running totals. Figure 16 uses the same data as Figure 15, but gives the cumulative number of student visits for tutoring. It is relatively easy to misinterpret a cumulative chart and to assume that the high point above each category, such as month, represents the total number of visits for tutoring *that month* rather than the running total. Thus, cumulative charts should be used sparingly.

Charts that depict quantitative predictions or relationships

1. Vertical bar charts depict the relationship between two variables, one of which can be quantitative or categorical and the other, quantitative. By convention, the horizontal x-axis usually depicts the categorical variable and the vertical y-axis the quantitative variable. Figure 17 presents an example; note that usual chart elements such as gridlines and x-axis labels are eliminated, but the message that more education is associated with higher family incomes is exceptionally clear.

2. Trend line charts show a straight "best fit" line drawn through data points to depict the overall trend, with the line drawn so as to

Figure 17
Vertical Bar

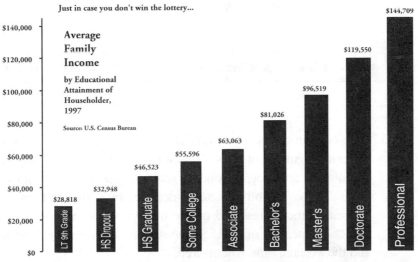

Just in case you don't win the lottery...

Average Family Income
by Educational Attainment of Householder, 1997

Source: U.S. Census Bureau

$28,818 — LT 9th Grade
$32,948 — HS Dropout
$46,523 — HS Graduate
$55,596 — Some College
$63,063 — Associate
$81,026 — Bachelor's
$96,519 — Master's
$119,550 — Doctorate
$144,709 — Professional

Published by Postsecondary Education OPPORTUNITY, P.O. Box 415, Oskaloosa, IA 52577, (515) 673-3401 minimize the distance from all points to the line. Trend line charts are especially useful for illustrating correlations between two interval variables. Scatterplots provide actual data points, often with a "best fit" line drawn through them. Figure 18 depicts grade point averages by age, showing clearly that the average grade point average (GPA) is higher for older students.[4]

Figure 18
Scatterplot with Best Fit Line
Grade Point Average and Age

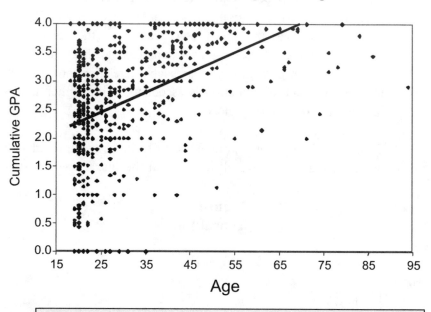

In fall 1998 the mean age of continuing students was 31; their mean GPA was 2.65

3. Line-column charts show the relationship between two factors that differ in magnitude or units of measurement. One factor is depicted by columns and a corresponding scale of measurement along one vertical axis. The other factor is depicted by a line, with its scale of measurement presented on the other vertical axis. Figure 19 depicts the percent of the U.S. population that volunteers, by age, and the average time volunteered.

Figure 19
Line-Column Chart with Two Factors

Percentage U.S. Population, by Age, Who Spend Time Each Week Volunteering
and Average Hours Per Week Volunteered

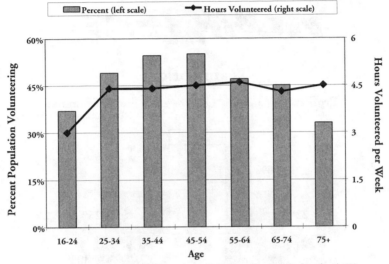

Source: *Giving and Volunteering in the United States*, data cited in Wall Street Journal, Monday, September 14, 1998

4. Butterfly charts show how two different ratings or scoring methods are used to examine the same variable. Figure 20 (p. 62) depicts data from the ACT Workkeys competency test. The vertical column gives the levels of importance or skill competency attached to the variable "teamwork." This is the scale. The horizontal bars on the left indicate the percent of jobs evaluated as requiring employees to work at the lowest level of teamwork (value < 3), the next highest level (value = 3), and so forth. The horizontal bars on the right depict the percentage of Workkeys test-takers who scored at each level of comptency on the teamwork test.

Charts that show other relationships: space, people, processes

The four categories of charts described above are based on variables where at least one variable is quantitative. Another broad category of charts depicts relationships among space, people, or processes. Sometimes a variable is quantitative, but it is displayed to reflect its association with a non-quantitative variable; a map illustrating states from which students come is an example. In higher education, a variety of relationship charts can provide useful presentations of information.

Figure 20
"Butterfly" Chart
Source: ACT - used with permission

Teamwork

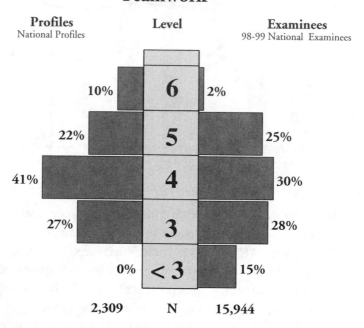

Profiles	Level	Examinees
National Profiles		98-99 National Examinees
10%	6	2%
22%	5	25%
41%	4	30%
27%	3	28%
0%	<3	15%
2,309	N	15,944

Note: Interpret data cautiously
as job profiles and examinees data
may not be representative of
jobs and examinee skills.

1. Flowcharts, process charts, or flow diagrams (the terms are used interchangeably) show the relationships or stages of a process, such as applying for financial aid. Various graphic conventions, such as arrows and connecting lines, reveal the direction of the flow. Figure 21 is a flowchart depicting a performance appraisal and review process.

2. Organization charts show the relationships among departments or

units within an organization, or among individuals occupying different positions in an organization. They are familiar, but can become complicated to execute when there are multiple reporting lines, cooperative but not direct line relationships, multi-functional task groups or teams, and multiple campuses where individuals report to leaders and superiors at another campus. Figure 22 (p. 64) is a relatively simple organizational chart.

Figure 21
Flow Chart

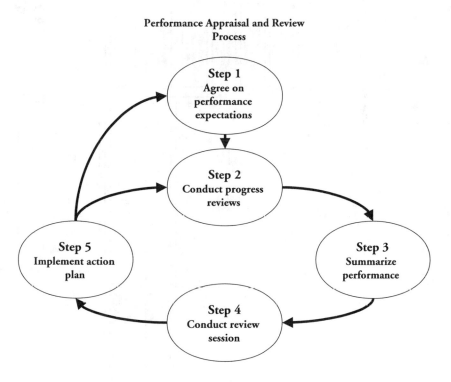

Performance Appraisal and Review Process

3. Schematics show the relationships of theoretical concepts, functions, or interactions. They are planning aids that provide analytical overviews of how offices or activities relate to one another in chronological or decision making, or some other order. Schematics can be especially useful in planning new or remodeled facilities, by depicting what offices ought to be near each other physically. Physical proximity is determined by the actual flow of

Figure 22
Organization Chart

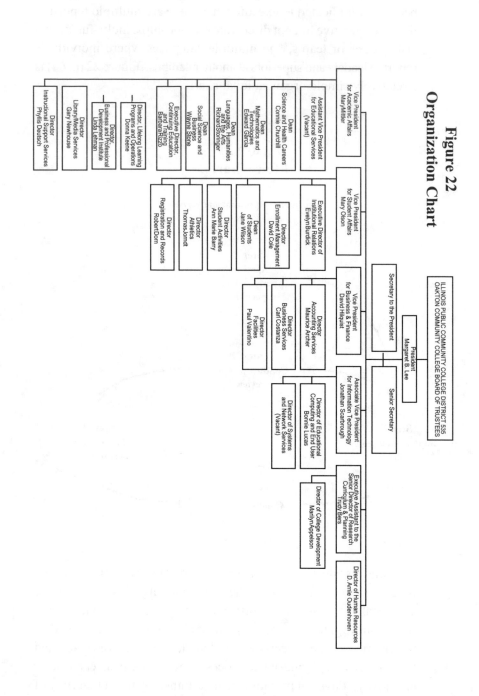

ILLINOIS PUBLIC COMMUNITY COLLEGE DISTRICT 535
OAKTON COMMUNITY COLLEGE BOARD OF TRUSTEES

President
Margaret B. Lee

Secretary to the President

Senior Secretary

Vice President for Academic Affairs
Mary Mittler

- Assistant Vice President for Educational Services (Vacant)
- Dean Science and Health Careers Connie Churchill
- Dean Mathematics and Technologies Edward Garcia
- Dean Languages, Humanities and the Arts Richard Storinger
- Dean Social Science and Business Wayne Stone
- Executive Director, Continuing Education and Training Barbara Rizzo
- Director, Lifelong Learning Programs and Operations Donna Keene
- Director Business and Professional Development Institute Linda Lehman
- Director Library/Media Services Gary Newhouse
- Director Instructional Support Services Phyllis Deutsch

Vice President for Student Affairs
Mary Olson

- Executive Director of Institutional Relations Evelyn Burdick
- Director Enrollment Management David Cole
- Dean of Students Jane Wilson
- Director Student Activities Ann Marie Barry
- Director Athletics Thomas Jorndt
- Director Registration and Records Robert Dorn

Vice President for Business & Finance
David Hilquist

- Director Accounting Services Maurice Archer
- Director Business Services Carl Costanza
- Director Facilities Paul Valentino

Associate Vice President for Information Technology
Jonathan Scarbrough

- Director of Educational Computing and End User Bonnie Lucas
- Director of Systems and Network Services (Vacant)

Executive Assistant to the Senior Director of Research, Curriculum & Planning
Trudy Bers

- Director of College Development Marilyn Appelson
- Director of Human Resources D. Arnie Oudenhoven

64

work. The schematic in Figure 23 shows how offices within College Learning Services at Pima Community College are both functionally and physically related. In planning for construction or remodeling, schematics are prepared to clarify and provide information to architects before they begin more detailed drawings or blueprints.

Figure 23
Schematic

Source: Robert Earl, Pima Community College, Facilities Planning, Tucson, Arizona.

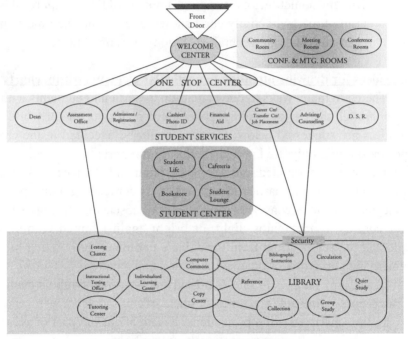

COLLEGE LEARNING SERVICES
MAJOR FUNCTION ADJACENCY DIAGRAM
Colors Represent Major Functional Groupings.
Circles Represent Major Functions.
Lines Represent a Strong Relationship Between Functions.

4. Time-and-activity charts are often used to illustrate the time frame within which discrete activities or stages of a more complex project will be undertaken. The total time for a project is reflected on the horizontal axis, while the vertical axis lists each activity beginning with the first. The amount of time each activity is expected to take is then shown on the horizontal axis, often by a narrow horizontal bar that begins and ends at the projected start and completion date

of that activity. Variations of time-and-activity charts include Gantt diagrams, decision trees, and Critical Path Method (CPM) and Program Evaluation Review Technique (PERT) charts. Gantt diagrams break processes into coherent segments that bring greater clarity to those attempting to understand or affect the process. Decision trees dispense with the time line, ending each discrete activity or event with a yes or no decision; either decision then leads to a distinct activity or event. CPM and PERT charts are especially useful for planning complex projects that require involvement from multiple units and comprise activities that take different, sometimes overlapping, amounts of time. Figure 24 is a simple-time-and-activity chart showing tasks and the time frame for implementing a general education assessment project.

Some ideas for drawing attention to particular elements within charts

There are many ways to draw attention to particular elements within charts through the use of shading, pattern, color, design, and artwork. A few ideas are suggested below; they can easily be executed in the chart types most commonly used in higher education reports.

Pie charts are divided into segments, often called slices or wedges. To focus attention on a particular segment, consider leaving it out entirely (the segment becomes conspicuous because of its absence), or using a strong color contrast (dark against light, or bright against muted colors), or exploding the segment out from the circle's perimeter, or pointing to the segment with an arrow or other symbol, or using a pattern.

Transform plain bars into pictorially descriptive symbols such as mortar boards to illustrate graduates, or stacks of coins to illustrate revenues.

In line charts showing projections, if data about the past or present are the focus, make the line projecting the future lighter in color, thickness, and/or weight (e.g., dots or dashes rather than a full line). If data about projections are the focus, then make the line projecting the future darker, brighter, thicker, or of heavier weight.

Arrows help to convey meaning visually. White (1984) provides a particularly useful description and illustrations of arrow designs and the meanings they impart. Arrows pointing right show foreword movement, positives, flow, or good. Conversely, arrows pointing left show backward movement, negatives, resistance, or bad. Arrows pointing up reflect increases, or good, while arrows pointing downward show falling, declines, or bad (though some declines are, in fact, good, e.g., declines in deficits).

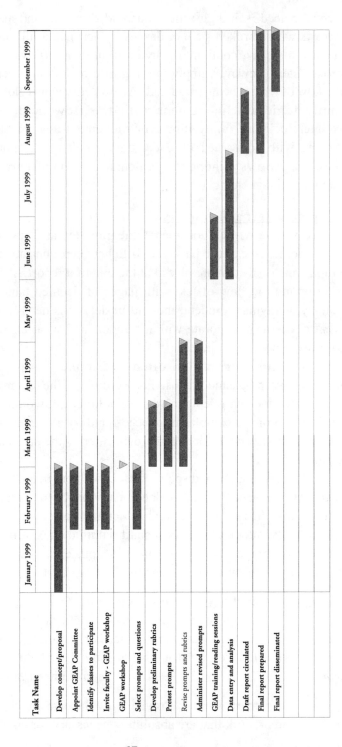

Figure 24
Time and Activity Chart
General Education Assessment Project

Arrows placed at an angle reflect the trend, direction, and speed of a change. Arrows with a broken stem or dashes, rather than a full line for the stem, suggest a steady, continuous, rhythmic motion; arrows with an uneven, broken stem, however, imply missing information or a deliberate stop in the flow of what is being presented. Arrows curved in a clockwise direction imply logic and movement with the flow, and arrows curved counterclockwise imply illogic or movement against the mainstream. Arrows with points at both ends suggest balance, dichotomy, or equal pressure. Arrows pointing at a particular segment of a graph draw special attention to that element.

Integrating text and graphics

Effective written documents integrate text and graphics. It annoys the reader to have to flip back and forth between a narrative and important graphic materials that are placed at the end of a report. At the same time, interrupting the flow of text with pages of detailed tables and charts is equally annoying. Prudent, thoughtful decisions need to be made about what charts to incorporate within a report and what charts can be more usefully appended at the end.

A simple suggestion, often overlooked, is to use consistent terminology in text and graphs. For example, if the text refers to program completers, the chart depicting data should too. It would be confusing to read about program completers in the text and see a chart depicting graduates when the two ways of presenting data refer to the same concept or data element.

If tables or graphic displays must be laid out in landscape rather than portrait style, place them in the document with the top of the display on the left to allow the reader to rotate the document clockwise.

Finally, attempt to imbed a chart within the text after not before, the pertinent narrative. If this is not possible, place the chart on the next page following the narrative or in an appendix or exhibit.

Some basic guidelines for presenting charts

This section provides some basic guidelines for presenting charts, with hard copy, transparencies, slides, or computer displays. These guidelines are derived from a number of sources, including Kosslyn (1994), Mims (1987), Tufte (1983, 1990, 1997), and White (1984).

1. Keep charts simple. Provide only the data, labels, titles, symbols and artwork that are absolutely necessary for conveying data and

information in an easy to grasp, memorable fashion. In other words, do not be seduced by graphical glitz.

2. Present variables according to some logic or organizing principle, such as size, date, or geographic region. The logic used depends on the subject and the major point(s) being illustrated. Sometimes presenting the same data sorted by different qualities on different charts is useful. For example, presenting enrollment by students' home states in descending order for number of students from each state emphasizes the most important feeder states for an institution. Presenting the same data ordered alphabetically by states make it easy for the reader to identify the importance of any specific state as a feeder to the institution.

3. When presenting several charts to compare information, keep display techniques comparable. For example, to use two pie charts to show the percent of revenue from various sources at different times, be sure to position the same source as much as possible in the same general quadrant, array sources in the same order around the chart, and use the same color or pattern for each source in both charts.

4. Use common sense to determine the use of grid marks, tick marks, and labels. Grid marks should normally be light in color or weight. Labels should be short and easy to read.

5. When using bar or column charts, place the dominant element at the bottom or left so it acts as a visual base.

6. To emphasize trends with column charts, join segments of adjacent bars or columns with lines. Also, put the segments that change the least amount at the bottom. This technique should be used cautiously, however, because sometimes the technique of joining segments suggests a three-dimensional perspective that inaccurately portrays the data.

7. Avoid using three-dimensions if only two dimensions are being portrayed. Three-dimensional graphics look sophisticated but are usually difficult to interpret. This rule is among the most frequently violated rules for presenting charts. Figure 25 (p.70) presents what is among the most common graphs used, a three-dimensional pie, to show sources of revenue for a college. Ironically there are not

three dimensions of data. Indeed, the three-dimensional display visually exaggerates contributions from tuition and fees and the state because these slices take more space than would be the case in a simple pie chart.

8. Follow conventions for constructing axes. Time is arrayed on the horizontal x-axis from left (past or present) to right (present or future). Quantity is tied to the vertical y-axis, with decreases or negative numbers arrayed downward and increases or positive numbers arrayed upward.

9. Use a maximum of six segments in a pie chart; explode a maximum of 25% of the wedges (ideally, then, no more than one wedge in a six-segment pie). Arrange wedges in a simple progression, usually by size, in a clockwise rotation.

10. Use no more than five or six data series on any single line graph.

11. Be very cautious about converting data into pictures; for example, it is difficult to adjust the size of a mortar board picture to reflect actual changes in numbers of graduates.

Figure 25
Three Dimension Pie Chart

Sources of Revenue - FY 1997

The real question is: What does 3-D add?

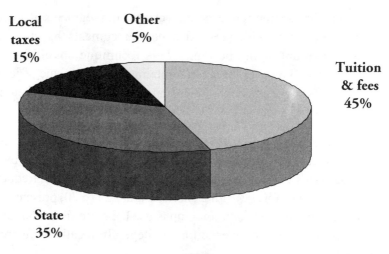

Local taxes 15%

Other 5%

Tuition & fees 45%

State 35%

Conclusion

Many of the guidelines and suggestions presented above are premised on common sense or basic knowledge about how humans perceive images and color. But sometimes common sense and basic knowledge collide with what have come to be expected formats for "sophisticated" presentations. As computer application packages have made it easy to create multi-dimensional charts with varied fonts, colors, symbols, artwork, and backgrounds, researchers and their audiences have come to expect more variation and visual elements in charts. Audiences may be disappointed by simple graphics that actually do a better job of illustrating data and information.

Effective reporting demands a judicious use of tools to enhance graphic displays, thoughtful simplicity of presentations, unwavering focus on the audiences for whom reports are intended, and prudence in the use of the elaborate presentation tools so readily available.

Chapter 7
Visual Presentation Modes - Transparencies, Slides, and Computer Screens

The overall communication and design principles discussed above apply to all communications media. However, there are some additional factors that affect the quality and utility of each medium and should be considered as visuals transformed for the written page, transparencies, slides, and computer screens. The World Wide Web (WWW), the newest mode of communicating, also deserves attention.

Transparencies, Slides, and Computer Presentations

The two most common ways of communicating messages in presentations are transparencies and slides, although computer presentation packages seem rapidly to be supplanting slides. Fink (1995) provides a useful comparison of the advantages and disadvantages of transparencies and slides, some of which are dependent on the presentation site. His comments are germane for computer presentations, as well. For example, where overhead projectors and screens or blank walls are routinely available, transparencies can be used without having to bring in other equipment. In many locations and at many conferences, overheads and screens are available without charge or pre-arrangement, but slide projectors, computers, video projection systems, and high resolution overhead projectors are not. Additional charges for this equipment can drive up presentation costs well beyond the benefits that accrue from using technology. While prices of laptop computers and personal LCD projectors are declining dramatically, it can still cost upwards of $4,000 to acquire this equipment. Consequently, it is not realistic to assume all IR offices will be able to have their own equipment to bring to presentations. At the same time, it may be useful for IR offices to explore acquiring equipment for the office or to be shared among several offices.

Slides and transparencies require advanced preparation time and do not permit the speaker to make changes during the presentation itself. Computer presentations can be modified continuously and also may appear more professional than transparencies or slides. However, equipment failures or bad lighting can substantially degrade the quality of computer presentations.

A transparency or slide (including both the traditional slide and the computer presentation slide) should contain just one main concept or figure. The number of lines should be limited to six, and the number of words per line should be limited to six or seven. Use phrases rather than sentences, and highlight key words or points with color, underlining, bullets, or other simple visual tools. Allow the audience at least one to two minutes per transparency or slide. If there is down time without an appropriate visual display during a presentation, consider using a blank transparency, or slide rather than turning on and off the projector, because changing lights can be distracting.

For slides, minimum letter height should be .5 mm, bold type. Slides with a blue or black background and white or other light type are most effective and easiest to read. Use no more than four colors per slide.

White (1984) provides useful information guiding the production of charts for slides or transparencies. Unfortunately, his book was written before microcomputer graphic and presentation programs became so widely available, so it does not contain references to this medium. He does present information about preparing visuals for television screens. The standardized image area in a 35mm slide is approximately seven-eighths of an inch high by one-and-a-quarter inches wide. To prepare images to be projected on a slide, then, all material must be contained within a rectangular configuration that conforms to this proportion, for example, five-and-a-quarter inches high by seven-and-a-half inches wide.

The opening on most overhead projectors is 10 inches by 10 inches, accommodating both horizontal and vertical displays. Allowing for frames or sleeves, letters and displays should be confined to a space measuring no more than seven-and-a-half inches by nine-and-a-half inches.

Television screens are proportioned differently from 35mm slides. In the latter, the shape proportion is about 3:4.5, while the proportion for television screens is 3:4. Moreover, because the outer edges of displays on screens sometimes disappear, the width of a presentation designed for screens is narrower than for slide usage alone; thus, to be safe, the display area should be made somewhat smaller all around. Differences in screen resolution and the quality of LCD panels, high resolution overheads, and other equipment provide additional challenges in preparing materials for computer or television display.

It should be noted that presentation software packages include many design templates. These purport to have built-in design elements and font sizes that conform, in most cases, with "best practice" guidelines, though this claim is sometimes disputed. One can begin with a prepackaged design template and make changes to conform to an office, institutional, or other preferred design standard. For example, institutional components such as logos or colors can be incorporated into standard designs.

What is the safest course of action to take in designing presentations for transparencies, slides, and computer presentations when one is not sure what presentation medium will be used? Use the common sense design principles suggested throughout this monograph, use larger fonts and a minimum number of words, minimize clutter and "chartjunk," and think about the presentations that have worked or not worked for you as a member of an audience.

The World Wide Web[5]

The WWW is the newest medium for disseminating reports and presentations. Rapid changes in technology and software for creating Web pages will soon make any material in this monograph about the actual creation of pages quickly obsolete. Therefore, in this section some broad suggestions are provided. Those interested in creating or updating Web pages should consult with campus staff who are knowledgeable about resources already available or compatible with campus computer systems.

Some principles guiding visual presentations in other media are applicable to Web pages as well, but some are not. For example, on the Web it is imperative to put key information on the first viewable page, without requiring scrolling. Second, on the Web more than with other media, the initial impression is critical. The page must be attractive and visually interesting or the viewer will move to another site immediately. Because it is possible to make sites attractive, this has become an expectation. Part of what makes a site visually attractive is the effective use of color, fonts, and graphics. It is important to realize that different browsers display the same color number differently. For example, a beige color on one browser appears to be pink on another; this not only changes the appearance, it also changes the tone, implying a soft, friendly, even feminine quality, rather than an impersonal, professional, even neutral one.

Graphics are expected, but must be in files that download rapidly. The compression format used by the file structure affects download time; the same graphic will yield different file sizes if saved in .bmp, .gif, or .jmp format. The most economical format is .gif. Another consideration relates to speed of the connection. If many users are likely to be accessing a Web-based presentation through telephone line connections, limited graphics should be employed, or two versions of the presentation might be created, one for high speed connections and one with fewer graphics for slower connections.

It is probably safe to assume that most people are now using one of the two standard browsers: Netscape or Microsoft Internet Explorer. Compatibility is moving from font and color support issues toward file compatibility issues. Web-based presentations should be tested on each of the currently popular browsers, and instructions or guidelines suggested to assist viewers.

Before beginning to design Web pages, researchers must determine the extent to which their pages need to conform to or be part of a more global site, such as a college or university Web site. Being part of such a site may provide excellent templates for Web page design, but can also limit options available to a specific office or person. Researchers must also define goals for their Web pages. This means determining the purpose of the pages, audiences, information to be conveyed, organization of the information, ways to attract users, and technical issues that can facilitate or impede use of the site.

It is also important to remember that Web site "attendees" are able to skim, focus on content based on personal or interests, and progress through the site in a non-sequential manner. This is different from attendees at traditional presentations, who are captive audiences forced to adhere to the timing and information sequences of the presenters.

Tufte (1998) says that people come to a Web site for content, not for cute icons, movements, and so forth. The main user activity at a Web site is flight from it, with download time generally exceeding the time of the visit itself. Flight occurs because the viewer does not know immediately what is available on the Web site. Furthermore, according to Tufte, a Web site can effectively contain many more than the five to nine choices typically available. He says that viewers can quickly scan through hundreds of items. The commonly accepted guidelines of chunking into groups of four as well as presenting no more than seven-eight ideas are related to memory, not to scanning.

Effective Web pages designers:

1. Provide links to other sites with relevant information.

2. Use consistent terminology throughout the Web pages.

3. Use the same icons throughout the presentation.

4. Use the same banner or identifying information on each page.

5. Use consistent layouts on each page.

6. Enable viewers to move back to the home page from each separate page, with the icon or words for moving back located in the same location on each page.

7. Include graphics only if they relate to content.

8. Alternate text with graphics.

9. Use colors that can be discriminated from each other.

10. Design each page so that it can stand alone.

Nielsen (1996) offers a useful list of 10 mistakes commonly made in Web design. As technology advances, some of these may no longer be relevant. Nielsen's list includes the following:

1. Frames, which are frequently confusing or do not work well. [Note: as of late 1998, frames operate more smoothly and may be the most effective presentation for large Web sites.]

2. "Bleeding-edge" technology, which is the very latest Web technology that may not be secure and will alienate users if the site crashes.

3. Scrolling text and running animations, which have an overpowering effect; users need some peace to actually read the text.

4. Complex URL's, which impede inferring the structure of the site and can be difficult for users to type.

5. Orphan pages that do not give users a way back to the site.

6. Long scrolling pages. Only 10% of users will scroll, and many of them get lost in the process.

7. Lack of navigation support, such as a site map, consistent structure, and search capability. Let users know where they are and where they can go.

8. Non-standard link colors. Unused links should be blue; used links should be purple or red. [As of late 1998, use of other colors for

links has become more frequent. As long as they are consistent within a Web site and remain true to the page design scheme, other color choices can be effective.]

9. Outdated information. Maintaining a site is frequently far more burdensome than creating it.

10. Long download times. Try to keep download times to 10 seconds or less.

The creation and maintenance of Web pages, as well as making reports and graphic displays available through the Web, bring new challenges and opportunities for effective communications. An immediate point of confusion regarding effective reporting is the consideration of how best to use the Web to present a specific report or topic, and how best to use it for presenting the broader work of the IR office.

Enthusiasm for the Web as a sole source for communications needs to be tempered with reality checks. For example, does one's audience have access to and actually make use of the Web? In the late 1990's, many people have access to the Web, but for a variety of reasons, do not use it on a regular basis. What browser is the primary audience most likely to be using? This will dictate the browser for which the Web site should be written. Is a written document appropriate for posting at a Web site? Does it contain sensitive information that should be limited in distribution? Is it in a format that will appear professional and be readable when downloaded at a remote site? How much time will it take to create and maintain an up-to-date site, and is this the best use of staff time? Does the current culture of the institution support use of the Web as the sole or dominant mode of internal communications? How much should use of the Internet replace other means of communicating, including in-person meetings, telephone calls, and traditional written memoranda? Will the institutional research office be perceived as unprofessional or out-of-date if the Web is not used for communication?

There are no absolute answers for these questions, but they need to be considered, and thoughtful decisions need to be made about using the Web — in addition to or in place of more traditional means of communicating. Use of — the Web by itself does not guarantee effective communication, absent adherence to the guidelines and principles of effective communication.

Chapter 8
Oral Reports

While much of this monograph is devoted to preparing reports that will be read and seen, it is important, as well, to be aware of the elements of effective oral reports. Whether presented as formal programs to large audiences, to small groups of colleagues in informal settings, or to audiences and in settings that vary between these extremes, certain ingredients enhance or detract from the quality of oral reports.

Imbedded in this chapter is an assumption: most institutional researchers will have had little formal training or professional development assistance in preparing and presenting oral reports and presentations. Thus the purpose of this chapter is to provide some basic principles and guidelines for oral reports. Participating in a workshop that includes experiences in making oral presentations, preferably videotaping them to permit critiques, is a better alternative to acquiring oral presentation skills than reading about them. However, a written document can provide some basic information in the absence of, or as a reinforcement to, an active learning option.

The Process of Oral Presentations

Beebe and Beebe (1997) outline steps in the speechmaking process. Although oral presentations of research material are not typically viewed as "speeches" per se, the tasks of formulating and delivering effective speeches are to those involved in giving any oral presentation of data and information. The steps are:

1. Consider the audience. This is the central focus because needs, attitudes, positions, values, level of knowledge, interest in the topic, and other characteristics should influence decisions made in every subsequent step.

2. Select and narrow the topic. Results of a research project may be the obvious topic, but many major topics include a number of subtopics, and audience characteristics may influence which ones to select or emphasize for the specific presentation. For example, when giving results of a student survey to an internal audience, there may be little need to describe the instituiton; but for an external audience, such a description may be essential to help them understand the setting within which the research took place.

3. Determine the purpose. The general purposes for oral presentations are usually to inform, to persuade, or to entertain. Information and, to a lesser extent, persuasion, are usually the purposes germane for institutional researchers, but sprinkling some humor into a presentation is often an excellent technique for keeping the audience's attention and for strengthening their ability to recall points made in the presentation. It is useful to ask, "What do I want my audience to know, to believe, or to do as a result of my oral presentation?" The answer to this question is not always obvious but, once clarified, can serve as an extremely useful reference point in developing the remainder of the presentation.

4. Develop the central idea of the presentation and then the key points to be made.

5. Gather or prepare appropriate verbal and visual supporting materials. These may include quotations, stories or narratives to illustrate key points, or even personal experiences of the institutional researcher or colleagues that are relevant to the topic. Visual materials can include handouts, transparencies, flip-charts, and traditional or computer presentation slides. In 1998, Tufte presented a full-day workshop on graphic presentations of data and information to an audience of over 1,000 gathered in a hotel ballroom in Chicago. Except for showing some short films at the end of the day, he did not use any transparencies, computer projections, or slides. Instead, he provided copies of his books as part of the registration. He asked his audience to turn to a specific page in a book and to look at a particular graphic or photograph. He then explained the key features of the graphic and why the depiction was especially good (or bad). This was a remarkably effective technique, although it was low-tech and required no equipment.

6. Organize the presentation. Every presentation should have an introduction, body, and conclusion. More specifically, a presentation should have a central idea, or one-sentence summary of the talk itself; an introduction, even an attention-catching opinion line or anecdote; a preview of major ideas; a statement telling the audience why they should listen; a body, with main and supporting ideas; and a conclusion that summarizes the major ideas and perhaps tells the audience what they might or should do next.

7. Rehearse the presentation.

8. Deliver the presentation.

Developing Confidence

Anxiety is one of the foremost impediments to giving effective oral presentations. Few institutional researchers are trained presenters, and even those who generally feel comfortable giving presentations to small groups of colleagues may be intimated by larger audiences or groups with whom they are unfamiliar. The following recommendations from Beebe and Beebe (1997) are useful tools for building confidence before giving an oral presentation.

1. Know the audience.

2. Be prepared, especially with a logically coherent outline that includes transitional phrases and summaries.

3. Select an appropriate topic or topics from the research.

4. Recreate the environment within which the presentation will be given; that is, try to imagine what the room will look like, its size, the arrangement of furniture and equipment, appropriate dress, whether or not a microphone will be used, and so forth.

5. Know the introduction and conclusion, even if the body of the presentation will be more spontaneous.

6. Imagine a calm, orderly presentation delivered in a confident, smooth manner.

7. Use deep breathing techniques; nervous speakers tend to take short, shallow breaths. Slowly inhale and exhale before beginning the presentation.

8. Act calm to feel calm. Arrive early to avoid a last minute rush, do not fidget, walk slowly to the podium.

9. Focus on the presentation content, not on fear.

10. Seek opportunities to present. Try out a major presentation before a small audience, perhaps colleagues or staff members at the office.

Virtually every college or university has a speech department or faculty who teach public speaking. Consider seeking help from a faculty member in crafting and rehearsing major oral presentations. Doing so can be useful, not just to improve organization and delivery, but also as a way to test out feedback on content from an individual who may share many similarities with the audience to whom the presentation will ultimately be made.

Assessing and Responding to the Audience During the Presentation

A crucial difference between reporting via paper or electronic means and reporting orally is the immediacy of audience response. Effective oral presentations frequently require the presenter to make real-time, instant modifications in the material or delivery to accommodate audience responsiveness, or lack thereof. This is not to say the content itself would be dramatically changed, though certain topics or ideas may need expansion or reduction. Sometimes having more or less time than anticipated forces such immediate changes.

Beebe and Beebe (1997) offer suggestions about adapting to the audience during the course of a presentation. They suggests presenters:

- Retain eye contact. A clear sign of audience disengagement is when members begin looking down or away.

- Look at facial expressions. Frozen, unresponsive looks suggest lack of attention or interest. However, some cultures are less likely to display expression even when members are highly attentive, and professionals who work with teenagers often remark on the lack of affect displayed by many teen-agers during group meetings.

- Observe body movements. Feet shuffling, drumming on a table, and restless moving about, are cues that the audience is losing interest or attention.

- Observe nonverbal responsiveness. Nods of agreement, applause, even laughter, are often signs the audience is paying attention.

- Listen for and to verbal responses. Asking questions, disagreeing with a point, even seeking agreement or clarification from a person seated adjacent, are also signals of interest or attention. Sometimes audience members will ask inappropriate questions or want to argue a point; an effective presenter responds briefly, but is careful not to let a single person or small group take over the presentation or divert it away from the topic.

Introductions to Oral Presentations

Effective oral presentations attract audience attention from the start, through effective introductions. Institutional researchers who do most of their reporting through formal, written documents may fail to recognize the power of an effective introduction to an oral presentation. In some ways these beginnings are like first impressions in any milieu: there is only one chance. This is different from written materials, where the reader can return often to the same document.

Beebe and Beebe (1997) suggest 10 ways of introducing oral presentations, acknowledging that each is not appropriate in all circumstances. Institutional researchers intent on making effective oral presentations may find it helpful to review the list and consider trying out a different approach to an oral presentation. The 10 ways are:

1. Illustration, such as a personal anecdote.

2. Startling fact or statistic.

3. Quotation.

4. Humor.

5. Questions.

6. References to historical events.

7. References to recent events.

8. Personal references, such as establishing expertise about the topic or revealing a knowledge of the audience.

9. References to the occasion.

10. References to preceding presentations, either at the same event or at other ones.

Conclusions to Oral Presentations

Just as the introduction is critical for attracting the audience, so the conclusion is equally important for leaving a strong, final impression, perhaps motivating the audience to take a certain action, to remember information, or to reconsider its attitudes about the topic. Beebe and Beebe (1997) assert that there are four purposes for an effective conclusion: summarizing the presentation, reemphasizing the main information in a memorable way, motivating the audience to respond, and bringing closure.

They suggest these techniques for achieving effective conclusions:

1. To summarize, tell the audience what you told them.

2. To reemphasize main information, use a well-worded closing phrase and provide a final example.

3. To motivate, urge the audience to think about or research the topic further, or to take specific actions.

4. To bring closure, refer back to the introduction, use a quotation, or make an appeal for action.

Effective Delivery

The real test of an oral presentation occurs when the presentation itself is made. Beebe and Beebe (1997) describe characteristics of effective deliveries and give suggestions for making high quality presentations. Characteristics and suggestions include:

1. Body language, which includes gestures, movement and posture.

   - Gestures can help to communicate, or can contradict, the meaning of oral statements. For example, when making three key points, holding up one, two, and then three fingers to emphasize each point. Gestures can be powerful substitutes or reinforcements for words. For example, to stop a discussion and refocus attention on the presenter, hold one hand high overhead. To use gestures well, a balance must be maintained between using a few or no gestures, and holding off from distracting gestures like flailing arms, overly repetitive movements, and gestures inconsistent with the message.

   - Movement refers to body language, such as walking around or staying in one place while delivering a presentation. In part, the use of movement is dictated by the physical set-up where the presentation is given; movement is obviously limited if one is seated or on a small platform. Walking into an audience to encourage dialog, taking a few steps to a different area to signify a change in topic, and moving out from behind a physical barrier to strengthen eye contact, are just some of the ways in which movement can improve the effectiveness of a presentation.

   - Posture refers to the way in which the body is carried. Slouching or leaning present very different images than standing erectly or sitting straight.

2. Eye contact. Maintaining eye contact with the audience improves the presentation's believability and credibility, opens communication, and enhances audience perception of the presenter's capability. Presenters who look at the ceiling, look over the heads of the audience, or look down continually, significantly and sometimes irreparably degrade the effectiveness of their presentations, no matter how strong the content may be.

3. Facial expression. Like body language and eye contact, facial expressions play an important role in conveying thoughts, ideas, attitudes, and knowledge of the presenter and, therefore, of the content of the presentation itself. Research has shown that although humans can make tens of thousands of facial expressions, unusually only six primary emotions are displayed: happiness, anger, surprise, sadness, disgust, and fear (p. 290).

4. Vocal delivery. Vocal delivery includes pitch, rate, volume, pronunciation, articulation, pauses, and general variation of voice (p. 291). Beebe and Beebe assert that in making effective oral presentations, presenters are obliged to speak to be understood, and to speak with variety.

   • Speaking to be understood includes speaking loudly enough to be heard, but not yelling, making words clear and distinct, and pronouncing words correctly. Mispronouncing key words can injure the presenter's credibility because it may be perceived by the audience that he or she does not understand what he or she is discussing.

   • Speaking with variety includes varying pitch, rate, and the use of pauses. Variety holds audience attention and also serves to emphasize or deemphasize key points.

5. Personal appearance. There is a great deal of evidence that personal appearance affects how an audience responds to a presenter and presentation. The level of formality of a presentation and the customs of the institution or the audience shape decisions about how to dress; usually a presenter for a formal presentation is advised

to wear clothing that is a step more formal than that which the audience wears.

Using Visual Aids

Much of this monograph is devoted to planning, organizing, and preparing effective visual aids such as charts, graphs, and figures. This section, drawn from Beebe and Beebe (1997), provides useful suggestions for incorporating visual aids into oral presentations.

1. Maintain eye contact with the audience even while using visual aids.

2. Explain the visual aids.

3. Do not pass visual aids among the audience.

4. Be judicious in distributing handouts before a presentation. If handouts are distributed, be sure they are related to the key points of the presentation, tell the audience what part(s) of the handouts to which you are referring, and consider preparing and telling the audience you will distribute a summary of key points after the presentation.

5. Use visual aids to influence audience attention. For example, remove a visual aid when the presentation moves to another point, turn the projector off when finished with visual aids, and consider asking a colleague to handle visual aids so the presenter can focus on the audience.

6. Have a back-up plan if technology fails.

Conclusion

A substantial body of research about effective communications presents overwhelming evidence that nonverbal communications, the nature of vocal deliveries, and the use of visual aids to supplement oral presentations have powerful impacts on the ways in which audiences perceive presentations with respect both to presenter and content. Effective reporting involves not just preparing formal written documents, but a host of other activities, formal and informal, written and oral, planned and spontaneous. Sharpening skills for oral presentations is an important, though often neglected, professional development task for effective institutional researchers.

Appendix A
Four Examples of Presenting the Same Data

Four examples of presenting the same data about credit hour enrollments are provided in Appendix A. Each should be considered a stand-alone document. While there is no right or wrong way to provide such data, the approaches do have attributes that may make them particularly useful or difficult for various audiences.

Appendix A-1 is a standard narrative in memo form. The memo explains the source of data and the variables included. Results are chunked into a paragraph that begins at the bottom of the page and continues to the next page. While the explanation of data and variables may be fairly clear, it will be difficult for the reader to grasp the findings because the paragraph is filled with numbers and there are no visual clues to help organize the data.

Appendix A-2 is a table that depicts the same data, with explanatory information in footnotes. The table is clean, easy to read, and gives precise data about each discipline as well as the business area as a whole.

Appendix A-3 is a vertical bar chart showing credits for each discipline for each year. The table lacks totals for the business area as a whole, and draws special attention to Computer Information Systems (CIS), which has substantially higher enrollments than the other disciplines. The chart does not permit the reader to distinguish easily the changes occurring in smaller disciplines such as Financial Information Services (FIS) or International Trade (ITR).

Appendix A-4 is a three-dimensional vertical bar chart depicting credits for each discipline for each year. The data do have three dimensions — number of credit hours, discipline, and year — so that in theory a three-dimensional chart should work. However, the display obscures rather than clarifies the data; it is nearly impossible to determine the number of credits by discipline and year; the disparity in credits among programs results in a flattening of bars in the small-credit programs, and the axis lines intended to guide the reader become almost dizzying in their affect. Enthusiasm for three-dimensional displays, even where there are three dimensions of data, need to be tempered by examining whether such depictions really help the reader. Appendix A-4 is a good illustration of the dangers of three-dimensional seduction.

The four different ways to present the same data illustrate a range of options available, and should also indicate that there is no single correct approach. Knowledge of the client, purpose, and audiences for a report, and the format in which it will be presented (e.g., written document, or in-person presentation using a computer presentation package), will influence which presentation form is most effective.

Appendix A - 1

Memo

Date: July 6, 1998   Copies to:

To: Dean of the Business Division

From: Director of Research

Subject: Credit Hour Enrollments in Business Disciplines

Based on your request, staff in the Research and Planning Office compiled data tabulating credit hour enrollments in business disciplines over the past three years. Data were drawn from the Student Management System, the College's official student database.

Disciplines examined were: accounting, business, computer information systems, financial services, hotel and hospitality management, international trade, management, marketing, office systems technology, and real estate.

Credit hour enrollments included in this project include enrollments as of the tenth day of the semester, which is the College's official census date, and enrollments in late-start classes, so long as the student was considered to be officially enrolled as of the census date of that class. Also, because students sometimes sit in a class without realizing they are not officially enrolled until later in the semester, staff also included enrollments of students who earned grades in the course (A, B, C, D, F) or received indicators reflecting enrollment (incompletes, withdrawals after tenth day, mid-term nonattendance, audit, and no grade from instructor).

Data were drawn from datasets specifically designed for research. These datasets are accessed through a program known as SQL. The value of these datasets is that they are "frozen," which means they do not change over time. Were research data to be extracted directly from "live" or "real time" datasets, there would be changes each time a topic was examined. The data are continually revised to reflect real-time enrollments.

Overall data reflect a decline in credit hours over the three-year period, from 27,136 to 25,875. This loss of 1,261 credits represents a decline of 4.6%. Changes within disciplines show a variety of patterns. Declines occurred in Accounting, (5,014 to 4,445 credits, a loss of 569 credits, or 11.3%), Business (3,399 to 2,922 credits, a loss of 477 credits, or 14%), Hotel and Hospitality Management (1,152 to 1,017 credits, a loss of 135 credits or 12%), International Trade (393 to 264 credits, a loss of 129 credits or 33%), Management (969 to 840 credits, a loss of 129 credits or 13.%), Office Systems Technology (4,421 to 3,653 credits, a loss of 1,291 credits or 30%), and Real Estate (1,025 to 800 credits, a loss of 225 credits or 22%). Increases occurred in Computer Information Systems (9,518 to 11,039 credits, a gain of 1,521 credits or 16%), Financial Services (282 to 386 credits, a gain of 104 credits or 37%), and Marketing (1,143 to 1,212 credits, a gain of 69 credits or .6%).

The loss of credits in Office Systems Technology was in part offset by enrollments in the new WWW courses, offered for the first time in 1997-98. There were 750 credit hours enrollments in these courses, which are offered cooperatively through Computer Information Systems and Office Systems Technology. Were the WWW credits added to the total, the 1997-98 total credit hours would be 26,625. The three-year change in credit would show a decline of only 511 credits, a 1.9% decline. WWW courses last year were taught primarily by OST faculty.

Please contact me if you would like additional information or analyses.

Appendix A - 2
Business Disciplines: Credit Hour Enrollments*
1995-96 through 1997-98

	1995-96	1996-97	1997-98	Change in credits over 3 years	Pct change over 3 years
Accounting	5,014	4,720	4,445	-569	-11.3
Business	3,399	3,261	2,922	-477	-14.0
Computer Info. Systems	9,518	10,227	11,039	1,521	16.0
Financial Services	282	279	386	104	36.9
Hospitality Management	1,152	1,005	1,017	-135	-11.7
International Trade	393	246	264	-129	-32.8
Management	969	858	840	-129	-13.3
Marketing	1,143	1,188	1,212	69	.06
Office Systems	4,241	3,653	2,950	-1,291	-30.4
Real Estate	1,025	716	800	-225	-22.0
TOTAL	27,136	26,153	25,875**	-1,261	-4.6

* Based on 10th day enrollments; enrollments in late-starting classes are included. Data source: Student Information Management System, downloaded to SQL as of tenth day and end-of-term.

** Courses in the World Wide Web (WWW) were offered for the first time in 1997-98, generating 750 credit hours. The WWW classes are offered cooperatively by Office Systems Technology (OST) and Computer Information Systems (CIS), but are taught primarily by OST faculty members. The WWW credit hours are not included in this total, nor in credit hour changes, nor in percent change over the three years. Were they added to the total, the 1997-98 total credit hours would be 26,625. The three-year change in credit would show a decline of only 511 credits, a 1.9 % decline.

Appendix A – 3
Vertical Cluster Bar Chart

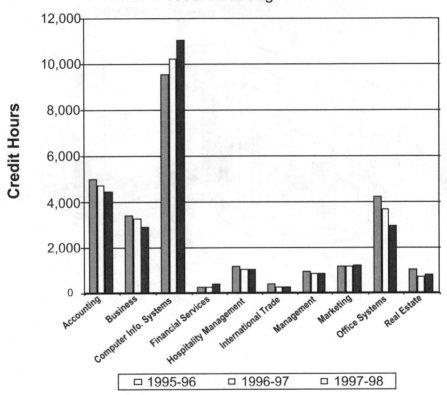

Business Discipline: Credit Hour Enrollments*
1995-96 through 1997-98

□ 1995-96   □ 1996-97   □ 1997-98

* Based on tenth day enrollments; enrollments in late-starting classes are included. Data source: Student Information Management System, downloaded to SQL as of tenth day and end-of-term. Courses in the WWW were offered for the first time in 1997-98, generating 750 credit hours. The WWW classes are offered cooperatively by Office Systems Technology (OST) and Computer Information Systems, but are taught primarily by OST faculty members. The WWW credit hours are not included in this graph.

Appendix A – 4
Three-Dimension Bar Chart

Business Disciplines:
Credit Hour Enrollments*
1995-96 through 1997-98

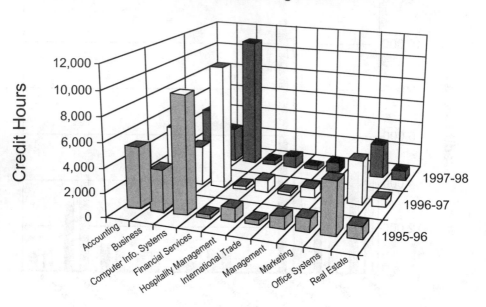

* Based on tenth day enrollments; enrollments in late-starting classes are included. Data source: Student Information Management System, downloaded to SQL as of tenth day and end-of-term. Courses in the WWW were offered for the first time in 1997-98, generating 750 credit hours. WWW classes are offered cooperatively by OST and CIS, but are taught primarily by OST faculty members. WWW credit hours are not included in this graph.

Glossary

Axes - Axes are the dimensions along which data are arrayed. Two-dimensional graphs are used to present two data elements. By convention, the horizontal x-axis, is used to show categorical, time, or independent variables. The vertical y-axis is used for responses or dependent values. A third variable can be displayed on the depth, or z-axis. This axis can also be used to show height or width.

Data annotations - Symbols, such as arrows, that call attention to a particular data point or part of a graph.

Data label - Text that names data points or series.

Data markers - Symbols used to show the location of a data point or series on a graph.

Data patterns - Designs used to differentiate parts or areas of a graph.

Data point - A plotting symbol (usually a dot) and axis designation (e.g., fiscal year).

Data region or plot - The rectangular area within axes, or the area within the circle of a pie chart, or the area encompassed by boundaries of a map, in which the data points or series are plotted.

Data series - A set of related points

Data shape - A shape depicted through two or three dimensions.

Footnotes - Explanatory information about some elements of the chart; placed below the data region.

Frames or boxes - Linear borders around the graph, incorporating legends, data, axis labels, and sometimes the graph title.

Grid or reference lines - Rules placed perpendicular to an axis that extend across the data region.

Key - A marker or symbol identical to the one used in the graph; presents the name of the associated variable, as well.

Labels (in text) - Text referring to axes, tick marks, gridlines, data points, and series; numbers used to identify amounts or categorical elements are treated as text, not values.

Leading - Pronounced "ledding," this is the space between lines; increasing leading where there is a great deal of text improves readability.

Legend - An area of the chart, presented either outside or inside the data region, that presents symbols, patterns, or colors and the names of their associated variables.

Patterns - Designs of lines, dashes, and dots that visually distinguish parts of a graph.

Picas - References to the width of type set in a line. Six picas equal one inch or 2.54 cm.

Points - Measures of the size (height) of print characters. Seventy-two points equals one inch or 2.54 cm; 12 points equal one-sixth of an inch or .423 cm.

Scale - Refers both to values and names along the axes and to the measurement units or distances between points along the axes.

Signs - Marks or language units that stand for or denote another thing; For example, a plus sign is used to denote addition or something positive. Signs are of four types: icons, indices, symbols, and metasymbols (Meggs, 1989). An icon resembles the thing it represents, an index is a factual or causal connection that points toward an object (smoke signifies a fire); a symbol has an arbitrary relationship with the object that is developed through knowledge and experience; and a metasymbol is a symbol that transcends the tangible realm, e.g. a dove symbolizes peace.

Tick marks - Short lines perpendicular to the axis that indicate regular intervals of the scale or categories of the axis.

Title - Label that gives the name of an individual chart or series of charts, usually shown above the chart. The APA convention is to refer to all tables as tables, and all graphs, pictures or drawings as figures.

Tones and colors - Visual mechanisms for conveying symbolic messages (red stands for stop or a deficit) or for differentiating parts of a graph.

Notes

[1] It is interesting to note, in contrast, that in a recent survey of institutional researchers (Knight, Coperthwaite & Moore, 1995), 81% indicated they were experts or to a large extent possessed the knowledge or skill of data presentation and reporting, and only 1% said they had difficulty in making research reports clearly understood. Knight, Coperthwaite & Moore suggest that the study might be limited by the absence of external, objective criteria for evaluating the degree to which respondents actually possess the relevant knowledge and skills they claim.

[2] For simplicity, the term "report" is used, but it should be interpreted to include graphical displays of data and information as well as oral presentations.

[3] The Integrated Postsecondary Education Data System (IPEDS) comprises annual surveys conducted by the National Center for Education Statistics, U.S. Department of Education, in compliance with the Center's mission "to collect, analyze, and disseminate statistics and other information related to education in the United States...," (P.L. 103-382, National Education Statistics Act of 1994, Sec. 404(a). Student-Right-to-Know (SRK) is the Student-Right-to-Know and Campus Security Act passed by Congress in 1991. It mandates that institutions eligible for participation in Title IV federal financial aid programs disclose graduation rates of their first-time, full-time students to their students and prospective students. Graduation Rate Survey (GRS) is the IPEDS Graduation Rate Survey. It collects data on the number of program completers by year of completion for a cohort of full-time, first-time students who entered the institution in a given year. The GRS was mandated in Section 485 of the Higher Education Act of 1965 (20 U.S.C. 1092) as amended. State Occupational Information Coordinating Committees (SOICCs) are interagency coordinating committees whose member agencies are the main producers and/or users of data on employment, education, and the labor market. The SOICC helps them identify issues of common concern and federal or state initiatives and resources that can be used to address information and career development needs in their state. SOICCs also participate in a national NOICC/SOICC Network, sharing products, best practices, and technical expertise.

[4] Some suggest the "best fit" line should be curvilinear to indicate an upper limit—in this case, the GPA of 4.0. Others argue that the straight line is more easily understood by those unfamiliar with statistical analyses.

[5] Victor Borden, Indiana University–Purdue University at Indianapolis, contributed significantly to this section.

References

Publication Manual of the American Psychological Association (4th ed.) (1994). Washington, DC: APA.

Aslanian, C, & Brickell, H. M. (1980) Americans in transition: Life changes as reasons for adult learning. New York: College Entrance Examination Board.

Astin, A. W. (1991). Assessment for excellence: The philosophy and practice of assessment and evaluation in higher education. New York: American Council on Education, Macmillan. (p. 264)

Barker, D., and Ott, M. (1990). Using Harvard Graphics for business presentations Boston, MA: Boyd & Frazer Publishing Company.

Beebe, S. A., and Beebe, S. J. (1997). Public speaking: An audience-centered approach (3rd ed). Boston: Allyn and Bacon.

Dale, E. (1969). Audiovisual methods in teaching. New York: Holt, Rinehart and Winston.

DiNucci, D., with Giudice, M. & Stiles, L., (1997). Elements of web design. Berkeley, CA: Peachpit Press.

Farquhar, A.B., & Farquhar H. (1891). Economic and industrial delusions: A discourse of the case for protection. New York, Putman.

Fink, A. (1995). How to report on surveys. Thousand Oaks, CA: Sage Publications.

Goldman, A. E. & McDonald, S. S. (1987). The group depth interview: Principles and practice. Englewood Cliffs, NJ: Prentice-Hall, Inc.

Houp, K. W., & Pearsall, T. E. (1992). Reporting technical information (7th ed.). New York: Macmillan.

Johnson, T. (November, 1994). Estimating the economic impact of a college or university on a nonlocal economy. Paper presented at the Association for the Study of Higher Education Annual Meeting. ERIC Document 375714.

Knight, W. E., Coperthwaite, C. A., & Moore, M. E. (May, 1995). Institutional research: Knowledge, skills, and obstacles to effectiveness. Paper presented at the Association of Institutional Research Annual Forum, Boston, MA.

Kosslyn, S. M. (1994). Elements of graph design. New York: W.H. Freeman and Company.

Krueger, R. A. (1994). Focus groups: A practical guide for applied research (2nd ed.). Thousand Oaks, CA: Sage Publications.

Krueger, R. A. (1998). Analyzing & reporting focus group results. Focus group kit 6. Thousand Oaks, CA: Sage Publications, Inc.

Lucas, R. (1996). Keynote address. The Association for Institutional Research Annual Forum. Albequerque, NM.

MacFarland, T. W., & Yates, J. M. (May, 1997). Presidents of independent colleges and universities judge the usefulness of the economic impact study. May Learning Associates, Boca Raton, FL. ERIC Document 409756.

Meggs, P. B. (1989). Type & image: The language of graphic design. New York: Van Nostrand Reinhold.

Middaugh, M. (1999). University of Delaware National Study of Instructional Costs and Productivity. [online] http://www.udel.edu/IR/cost/brochure.html. [1999, March 16]

Mims, R. Sue, ed. (1987). The design, production and use of computer graphics: A tutorial and resource guide. Tallahassee, FL: The Association for Institutional Research.

Nielsen, J. (1999). Top Ten Mistakes in Web Design. Jakob Nielsen's Alertbox for May 1996. [online] http://www.useit.com/alertbox/9605.html. [1999, February 3]

Scoville, R. (1988, September). Ten Graphs (and How to Use Them). PC World. pp. 216-219.

Seybert, J. A. (1994). Effective Reporting. Unpublished material prepared for The Association for Institutional Research Institute for Institutional Researchers. Tallahassee, FL.

Shannon, C.E., & Weaver, W. (1949). Mathematical theory of communication. Urbana, IL: University of Illinois Press.

Sinclair Community College (1997). Always on your side: An independent economic impact analysis. Dayton, OH.

Staley, C. M., & Stopke, J. (1990). Desktop design: Fundamentals of design for desktop publishing. Ann Arbor, MI: Promotional Perspectives.

Templeton, J. F. (1994). The focus group. Revised edition. Chicago, IL: Probus Publishing Company.

Terabian, K. L. (1987). A manual for writers of term papers, theses, and dissertations (5th ed.). Chicago, IL: The University of Chicago Press.

Tufte, E. R. (1983). The visual display of quantitative information. Cheshire, CT: Graphics Press.

Tufte, E. R. (1990). Envisioning information. Cheshire, CT: Graphics Press.

Tufte, Edward R. (1997). Visual Explanations. Cheshire, CT: Graphics Press.

Tufte, E. R. (1998, April). Presentation on Graphic Design. Chicago, IL.

Wainer, H. (1992, January-February). Understanding Graphs and Tables. Educational researcher, pp. 12-23.

Wallgren, Anders, Wallgren, Britt, Persson, Rolf, Jorner, Ulf, & Haaland, Jan-Aage (1996). Graphing statistics & data: Creating better charts. Thousand Oaks, CA: SAGE Publications.

Warren, J. (1985). Basic graphic design & paste-up: How to design and prepare artwork for printing. Cincinnati, OH: North Light Books.

West, S. (1991). Comping techniques: Visualizing and presenting graphic design ideas. New York: Watson-Guptill.

White, J. V. (1984). Using charts and graphs: 1000 ideas for visual persuasion. New York: R.R. Bowker Company.

Williams, R. (1996). Home sweet home page. Berkeley, CA: Peachpit Press.

Wurman, R. S. (1997). Information architects. New York: Graphis, Inc.